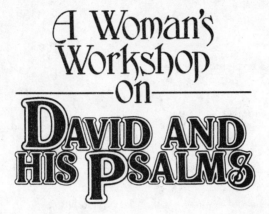

A Woman's
Workshop
—on—
DAVID AND
HIS PSALMS

Books in this series—

A Woman's Workshop on

DAVID AND HIS PSALMS

With Helps for Leaders

Carolyn Nystrom

Lamplighter Books Grand Rapids, Michigan
Zondervan Publishing House

A Woman's Workshop on David and His Psalms
Copyright © 1982 by The Zondervan Corporation
Grand Rapids, Michigan

Lamplighter Books are published by Zondervan
Publishing House, 1415 Lake Drive, S.E.,
Grand Rapids, Michigan 49506

Library of Congress Cataloging in Publication Data

Nystrom, Carolyn.
    A woman's workshop on David and his Psalms.

    (Woman's workshop series)
    Bibliography: p.
    Includes index.
    1. David, King of Israel. 2. Palestine—Kings and rulers—Biography. 3. Bible.
O.T.—Biography. 4. Bible. O.T. Psalms—Text-books. I. Title. II. Series.
BS580.D3N97   222'.40924 [B]   82-2703
ISBN 0-310-41931-X   AACR2

Edited by Louise Rock

Scripture passages are quoted from the *New International Version of the Bible*
(North American Edition), copyrighted © 1978 by The International Bible Society.

Printed in the United States of America

84 85 86 87 88 — 10 9 8 7 6 5 4

to
the forty-three men and women
who helped me try it out

CONTENTS

DAVID AND HIS PSALMS

Hot sun bakes the Judean hills. An old man slips through its small villages, hoping to escape notice. He can't. People whisper, "Samuel, why are you here? Where are you going?"

To these he announces, "I'm on my way to Bethlehem to make a sacrifice."

But others offer a quiet warning, "Careful, old man. Saul's men are everywhere." Samuel nods and hurries on.

Beneath his cloak, he carries a precious horn of oil. At God's command, this prophet must use the oil to anoint a new king. Yet the old king still reigns. And King Saul is a valiant warrior and a powerful ruler. He is also a madman. Samuel himself does not know whom God has appointed as king. But he does know that his trip is dangerous.

In this setting, David walks into the pages of Old Testament history—not as a great king acquiring an empire beyond Israel's farthest borders (though he becomes that later), but as a boy, a shepherd, underestimated by his father and scorned by his brothers. Even Samuel must wonder, "Can this boy David be king?"

God's response is simple. He reminds Samuel, "Man looks at the outward appearance, but the LORD looks at the heart."

Scripture gives its students a unique opportunity to capture God's view of David. His "outward appearance" (his life and actions) covers a massive expanse of text—some sixty chapters, told in graphic detail. We see David, a child in battle, killing a giant. We see him a royal aide to King Saul and bosom friend of Jonathan, Saul's son. And we see him spend years fleeing from Saul's attempts to murder him.

We see him eventually made king, and then expand Israel's borders beyond those of any time in history. We see David dance in worship, but we also see him plot adultery and murder. And we see him fall from his throne—a victim to his own son. In the end, we see David die: a good man, a sinful man, a forgiven man, a man of God. A person the New Testament calls, "a man after God's own heart."

But beyond these sixty chapters of vivid action, Scripture gives us another view of David. We also come to know David's heart. David wrote at least seventy-three psalms. These psalms are prayers, outpourings of his inner person as he talks with and pleads with and worships his God. Here we feel his words dance with praise. Or we picture him cringing with guilt. Or lashing out at his enemies. Or marveling at a God enormous enough to make the stars and yet care for the smallest fetus. We also hear him pleading, "Search me, O God, and know my heart . . . See if there is any offensive way in me."

This study guide will help you know David—outside and in. It will not tell you what the Scripture says. The Scripture speaks quite eloquently for itself. Instead this guide provides questions that will help you examine the Scripture—maybe even direct your attention to a few nuggets you might otherwise miss. Then the questions invite you to live out the implications of the passage. How might you think, believe, behave, as a result of its teachings?

Don't neglect the studies titled "Through the Week." Many of these quiet-time studies look at the Psalms (David's heart). While we cannot know exactly when David wrote many of these, every effort has been made to correlate the subject of each psalm with events in his life. They form a thread of worship interweaving the highs and lows of his experience. Don't miss praying David's prayers with him.

Enter the study of David with anticipation. Study with diligence. And emerge with joy. I did!

In His service,
Carolyn

I'VE JOINED THE GROUP. NOW WHAT?

You've joined a group of people who agree that the Bible is worth studying. For some it is the Word of God and therefore a standard for day-to-day decisions. Others may say the Bible is merely a collection of interesting teachings and tales, worthy of time and interest but not much more. You may place yourself at one end of this spectrum, or at the other end. Or you may fit somewhere in between. But you have one goal in common with the other people in your group: you believe that the Bible is worth your time, and you hope to enjoy studying it together.

To meet this goal, a few simple guidelines will prevent needless problems.

1. **Take a Bible with you.** Any modern translation is fine. Suggested versions include: Revised Standard Version, New American Standard Bible, Today's English Version, New International Version, Jerusalem Bible.

A few versions, however, do not work well in group Bible study. For beautiful language, the King James Version is unsurpassed. Yours may bear great sentimental value because it belonged to your grandmother. But if you use a King James, you will spend a great deal of effort translating the Elizabethan English into today's phrasing, perhaps losing valuable meaning in the process.

Paraphrases like Living Bible, Phillips, and Amplified are especially helpful in private devotions, but they lack the accuracy of a translation by Bible scholars. Therefore leave these at home on Bible study day.

If you would like to match the phrasing of the questions in this guide, use the New International Version. If, however, you fear that any Bible is far too difficult for you to understand, try Today's English Version. This easy-to-read translation is certain to change your mind.

2. **Arrive at Bible study on time.** You'll feel as if you're half a step behind throughout the entire session if you miss the Bible readings and the opening survey questions.

3. **Come prepared.** Six personal studies follow each group discussion in this guide. These studies form a bridge between each week's discussion. Don't stay home if you haven't done the work. But if you spend twenty minutes each day on these "Through the Week" assignments you will greatly increase the value you receive from studying David. Keep a notebook for these assignments. Then you'll have a written record of your personal growth.

Some people have trouble concentrating on a passage of Scripture if they read it for the first time during a group discussion. If you fall into that category, read it ahead of time while you are alone. But try to reserve final decisions about its meaning until you've had a chance to discuss it with the group.

4. **Call your hostess if you are going to be absent.** This

saves her setting a place for you if refreshments are served. It also frees the group to begin on time without waiting needlessly for you.

When you miss a group session, study the passage independently. David's life forms a story. You'll feel better able to participate when you return if you have studied the intervening material.

5. **Volunteer to be a hostess.** A quick way to feel as if you belong is to have the Bible study group meet at your house.

6. **Decide if you are a talker or a listener.** This is a discussion Bible study, and for a discussion to work well all persons should participate more or less equally. If you are a talker, count ten before you speak. Try waiting until several other people speak before you give your own point of view.

If you're a listener, remind yourself that just as you benefit from what others say, they profit from your ideas. Besides, your insights will mean more even to you if you put them into words and say them out loud. So take courage and speak.

7. **Keep on track.** This is a group responsibility. Remember that you are studying the life of David. Although a speech, magazine article, or some other book may be related, if brought into the conversation it will automatically take time away from the main object of your study: David. In the process, the whole group may go off into an interesting-but-time-consuming tangent, thereby making the leader's job more difficult.

While the Bible is consistent within itself and many excellent topical studies build on its consistency, the purpose of this study is to examine thoroughly David's life. Therefore cross referencing (comparing sections of Samuel with other portions of Scripture) will cause the same problems as any other tangent. In addition to confusing people who are unfamiliar with other parts of the Bible, cross referencing may cause you to miss the writer's intent in the passage before you.

Each Scripture passage is so laden with facts and ideas that you will be thoroughly challenged to straighten these out without turning to other sections of the Bible.

Naturally, once you have studied a section as a group, you may refer back to it. The writer assumed his readers had the earlier passage in mind before they read his next section.

8. **Help pace the study.** With the questions and your Bible in front of you, you can be aware of whether or not the study is progressing at an adequate pace. Each group member shares the responsibility of seeing that the entire passage is covered and the study brought to a profitable close.

9. **Don't criticize another church or religion.** You might find that the quiet person across the table attends that church—and she won't be back to your group.

10. **Get to know people in your group.** Call each other during the week, between meetings. Meet socially, share a car pool when convenient, offer to take in a meal if another group member is ill. You may discover that you have more in common than a willingness to study the Bible. Perhaps you'll add to your list of friends.

11. **Get ready to lead.** It doesn't take a mature Bible student to lead this study. Just asking the questions in this guide should prompt a thorough digging into the passage. Besides, you'll find a hefty section of leaders' notes in the back in case you feel a little insecure. So once you've attended the group a few times, sign up to lead a discussion. Remember, the leader learns more than anyone else.

ME, A LEADER?

Sure. Many Bible study groups share the responsibility of leading the discussion. Sooner or later your turn will come. Here are a few pointers to quell any rising panic and help you keep the group working together toward their common goal.

1. **Prepare well ahead of time.** A week or two in advance is not too much. Read the Scripture passage every day for several successive days. Go over the questions, writing out possible answers in your book. Check the Leaders' Notes at the back of the book for additional ideas, then read the questions again—several times—until the sequence and wording seem natural to you. Don't let yourself be caught during the study with that now-I-wonder-what-comes-next feeling. Take careful note of the major area of application. Try living it for a week. By then you will discover some of the difficulties others in your group will face when they try to do the same. Finally, pray. Ask God to lead you, as you lead the group. Ask Him to

make you sensitive to people, to the Scripture, and to Himself. Expect to grow. You will.

2. **Pace the study.** Begin on time. People have come for the purpose of studying the Bible. You don't need to apologize for that. At the appointed hour, simply announce that it is time to begin, open with prayer, and launch into the study.

Keep an eye on the clock throughout the study. These questions are geared to last for an hour to an hour and fifteen minutes. Don't spend forty-five minutes on the first three questions then have to rush through the rest. On the other hand, if the questions are moving by too quickly, the group is probably not discussing each one thoroughly enough. Slow down. Encourage people to interact with each other's ideas. Be sure they are working through all aspects of the question.

Then end—on time. Many people have other obligations immediately after the study and will appreciate a predictable closing time.

3. **Read the passage aloud by paragraphs—not verses.** Verse by verse reading causes a brief pause after each verse and breaks the flow of narrative, thereby making it harder to understand the total picture. So read by paragraphs.

4. **Ask; don't tell.** This study guide is designed for a discussion moderated by a leader. It is *not* a teacher's guide. When you lead the group, your job is like that of a traffic director. You gauge the flow of discussion, being careful that everyone gets a turn. You decide which topics will be treated in what order. You call a halt now and then to send traffic in a new direction. But you do not mount a soapbox and lecture.

Your job is to help each person in the group discover personally the meaning of the passage and to share that discovery with the others. Naturally, since you have prepared the lesson in advance, you will be tempted to tell them all you've learned. Resist this temptation until others have had a chance to discover the same thing. Then, if something is still missing, you may add your own insight to the collection.

5. **Avoid tangents.** The bane of any discussion group is the oh-so-interesting lure of a tangent. These are always time consuming and rarely as profitable as the planned study. A few red flags will warn you that a tangent is about to arise. They are, "My pastor says . . ."; "I read that . . ."; "The other day Suzie . . ."; "If we look at Ezekiel (or John, or Revelation) . . ."

If this occurs, politely listen to the first few sentences. If these confirm your suspicion that a tangent is indeed brewing, thank the person, then firmly but kindly direct attention back to the passage.

A leader does, however, need to be sensitive to pressing needs within a group. On rare occasions the tangent grows out of a need much more important than any pre-planned study can meet. In these cases, whisper a quick prayer for guidance, and follow the tangent.

6. **Talk about application.** Each study in this guide leads to a discussion that applies the point of the passage to real life. If you are short of time or if your group feels hesitant in talking about personal things, you'll entertain the thought of omitting these questions. But if you do, your group will lose the main purpose of the study. If God's Word is a book to live by, a few people in your group ought to be willing to talk about how they are going to live in response to it. Putting those intentions into words will strengthen their ability to live out the teachings. The listeners will be challenged to do the same.

So, always allow adequate time to talk over the application questions. Be prepared also to share the passage.

7. **Try a prayer 'n' share.** Many groups start their session with fifteen minutes of coffee, then hold a short time of sharing personal concerns, needs, and answers to prayer. Afterward, the group members pray briefly for each other, giving

thanks and praise, and asking together that God will meet the needs expressed. These short informal sentence prayers are much like casual sharing conversation. The group members simply turn their conversation away from each other and toward God. For many, this brief time of prayer becomes a weekly life line.

8. **Enjoy leading.** It's a big responsibility, but a rewarding one.

BIBLE STUDY SCHEDULE

Date	Passage	Leader	Hostess
	1 Samuel 16		
	1 Samuel 17		
	1 Samuel 20		
	1 Samuel 23–24		
	Psalm 62		
	1 Samuel 25		
	1 Samuel 31– 2 Samuel 2:7		
	2 Samuel 6		
	2 Samuel 7		
	2 Samuel 11–12		
	Psalm 32		
	2 Samuel 15–16		
	2 Samuel 18:1– 19:8		
	1 Chronicles 21		
	1 Chronicles 22, 28–29		
	Psalm 139		

Names and phone numbers:

PLEASE CALL HOSTESS IF YOU CANNOT ATTEND

A MAP FOR LESSONS 1–16

GESHUR

△ Mount Gilboa
Beth Shan●

●Jabesh Gilead

Great Sea
(Mediterranean)

ISRAEL

River Jordan

AMMON

Rabbah●

●Ramah
Baalah●   ●Jerusalem
Ekron●   ●Bahurim
Gath● ●Azekah   ●Bethlehem
●Socoh
●Keilah
●Hebron
Ziph● ●En Gedi
●Carmel
Maon●

Dead Sea

PHILISTINES

JUDAH

MOAB

0   5   10 miles

21

A MAP FOR THE "THROUGH THE WEEK" NARRATIVE

HAMATH

ARAM-ZOBAH

BETH-REHOB

ARAM-DAMASCUS

SIDONIANS

Tyre

Abel Beth Maacah

Great Sea (Mediterranean)

MAACAH

GESHUR

Helam

Shunem • Endor

Jezreel

△ Mount Gilboa

Tob

Jabesh Gilead

ISRAEL

Aphek

Mahanaim

GILEAD

AMMON

Baal Hazor • Gilgal

Gezer • Gibeon • Ramah • Jericho

Rabbah • Gibeah • Nob

Baal Perazim • Jerusalem

Gath • Bahurim

Adullam • Bethlehem

Hebron • Tekoa

Ziklag • Carmel

JUDAH

MOAB

0 10 20 miles

AMALEK

Horonaim

Valley of Salt

••• Extent of David's kingdom

--- Interior border

EDOM

22

1

IS ANYONE IN CHARGE UP THERE?

1 Samuel 16

The kingdom looked good to King Saul. Israel's first anointed king had so far been a rousing success. He'd won most of his battles against the nation's perennial enemies, the Philistines. He'd taken enough plunder to become rich. And he'd assembled a royal court. Not bad for a first king.

But there was that nagging prophet, Samuel. Samuel had anointed him king years back and ever since seemed to take it upon himself to speak out God's commands—as if he had orders from on high. But Saul had learned not to take the old man too seriously. "Samuel's probably just jealous that he and his 'word from the Lord' is no longer the top authority in Israel," Saul told himself.

Still, that last nasty confrontation with Samuel prickled at Saul's mind. Samuel's words, "The LORD has rejected you as king over Israel," had an ominous ring. And oddly enough, the old man had walked away sad.

Helps for leaders can be found at the back of the book.

Read aloud 1 Samuel 16:1–13.

1. What difficulties did Samuel have to overcome in order to carry out the job God assigned him? _____

    _____

    _____

2. What can you know of Samuel's personality from these verses? _____

    _____

    _____

3. What hints do you have here that God cares about His people? _____

    _____

4. Assume Jesse knew that Samuel was anointing one of his sons to be king. If you had been Jesse, what would you have felt during this experience? _____

    _____

    What would have been your temptation?

    _____

    _____

5. How might David's experience as a shepherd be of value to him when he becomes king? _____

    _____

    _____

    _____

6. How does this passage show God's values to be different from human values? _____

    _____

7. If you were to try to see people more the way God does, what would you do differently? _____

_____

_____

*8. If you made a concentrated effort to understand the inner person, with whom would your relationship be most improved? _____

Why? _____

_____

Read aloud 1 Samuel 16:14–23.

9. What evidence do you see that God prepared the way for David to be accepted into Saul's court?

_____

_____

_____

10. What was David's reputation with at least one of Saul's servants? _____

_____

How might these qualities help David in the job Saul gave him? _____

_____

_____

How might these same qualities help him in his future role as king? _____

_____

_____

_____
*optional question

11. What changes took place in Saul because the Spirit of the Lord had departed from him? _____

    _____

    _____

*12. Why might David and Saul each take the presence of God's Spirit seriously? _____

    _____

    _____

13. What evidence did you find in this chapter to support the claim that God is in control? _____

    _____

    _____

    _____

14. If you truly believed that God is in control, what effect would it have on the way you react to your present circumstances? _____

    _____

    _____

    _____

A Note About Through the Week

Do you have twenty minutes free time a day? If so, you can do each "Through the Week" study in this guide, beginning on the next page. These studies build on the group discussion you have just finished and lead into the next study. If you do them all, you will have studied David's whole life and known writings. Try keeping a "Through the Week" notebook.

THROUGH THE WEEK

Day 1
Read Psalm 23.

1. Find as many things as you can that David must have done for his sheep.
2. What human experiences might lead David to think of God as meeting those same needs in His people?
3. In what respect do you need God to be a shepherd to you right now?
4. Talk to Him about it. Then yield yourself to Him. Let God, your loving Shepherd, take care of you.

Day 2
Read again Psalm 23.

1. What does this psalm tell you about God's nature? List as many qualities as you can.
2. Under what circumstances do you value each of these characteristics in God?
3. Spend time meditating on who God is. Now thank and praise God for the qualities that make up His nature. Let your prayer worship God for what He has revealed to you of Himself.
4. Look ahead at your routine for the coming day. As much as you are able, dedicate these activities to God as a continuation of your worship.

Day 3
Read Psalm 19.

1. What does creation reveal about God? (See verses 1–6.)
2. What does Scripture add to this revelation of God's nature? (See verses 7–10.)

3. What is David's response to this knowledge? (See verses 11–14.)
4. In what ways has your experience shown that thoughts and words are connected?
5. Read verse 14 aloud as your prayer to God for the coming day.

Day 4
Read again Psalm 19.

1. How might David, the shepherd, have learned these truths about God?
2. According to this psalm, what does God give to His people? (List all that you can.)
3. To what extent are David's feelings about God's law different from yours?
4. If a person became exposed to God's Word but did not allow it to govern his life, what would he be missing?
5. Are there ways in which you are now rebelling against a written law of God? If so, admit this to God and ask His forgiveness. When you are able, pray David's prayer of verses 12b–13.

Day 5
Read 1 Samuel 15.

(This chapter records the last of a long series of confrontations between Samuel, God's prophet, and King Saul. It set the stage for the anointing of David.)

1. What did Saul do wrong? (Find all that you can.)
2. What appear to be Saul's reasons for disobeying God?
3. How does Samuel use his own torn robe as a symbol of the future?
4. Read slowly verses 22–23. When would you rather *give* something to God than *do* what He commands? Why?

5. Think of one difficult command that God gives you in Scripture. Write: God says to _____ (write your name), then record the command. Pray, asking God to point out every opportunity to obey this command today. Then ask His help as you try to follow it.

Day 6
Read Psalm 141.

1. Why might this prayer be appropriate for the time David spent serving in Saul's house?
2. What contrasts does David see between good and evil?
3. What steps does he plan that will put him on God's side?
4. When, this week, are you likely to feel surrounded by those who do not honor God? (One strong-minded person can "surround" you.) Talk to God about that time. Share with Him your temptations and fears in that setting. Then pray verses 3 and 4 as you ask His help.

2

ARE MY BATTLES GOD'S BATTLES?

1 Samuel 17

—You're at a school board meeting and doing your part to fight for, or against, sex education in the local high school.

—Your husband says, "No, I don't want you to join that weekly exercise class [or prayer group]. I work hard all day and shouldn't have to take care of kids when I get home."

—You've caught yourself at it again—stretching the truth to make a better story. You got an audience all right, but it's the third time this week you've fallen into the "lie trap." And just last week you promised God you'd try to lick this sin.

Battles: battles in the community, battles at home, battles within ourselves. We fight them every day. But are our battles God's battles? Which side are we on? And how can we know?

Read aloud 1 Samuel 17.

1. What details make this story come alive for you?

Helps for leaders can be found at the back of the book.

_____

_____

_____

_____

_____

2. What can you know from this chapter about the relationships within David's family? _____

_____

_____

3. How did David's conversation with Saul reveal a different person than his family perceived?

_____

_____

_____

4. How did David's knowledge of God affect his view of himself and his work? (Consider events only through verse 40.) _____

_____

_____

_____

5. What do you know about God that might help you attack a difficult task with confidence? _____

_____

_____

_____

_____

6. What was at stake when David went out against Goliath? _____

    _____

    _____

7. In what ways did David and Goliath appear to be mismatched? _____

    _____

    _____

    _____

8. What could those who witnessed the dialogue and battle know about David's God? _____

    _____

    _____

    _____

9. What would you like people who witness your battles to know of your God? _____

    _____

    _____

    _____

10. Mention one "battle" in which you are currently engaged. How might you fight this battle in God's name and by his methods? _____

    _____

    _____

    _____

THROUGH THE WEEK

Days 1 through 5
Psalms 124, 36, 29, 14 or 53, and 131.

Each of these psalms reveals God's power and authority in a conflict situation. No towering Goliath appears, yet we see God at war against the forces of evil, we see His authority over nature, and even over David himself.

Read aloud one psalm each day. Examine it for details by noting answers to the following questions. Then watch for opportunities throughout the day to thank and praise God with David for the qualities God reveals of Himself in that psalm.

1. What picture does this psalm paint in your mind?
2. What emotion does this imagery evoke?
3. In what ways does this psalm show God's authority?
4. What caution do you find here for the person who opposes God?
5. Find one sentence of this psalm that seems particularly appropriate to your present circumstances. Pray it to God.

Day 6
Read 1 Samuel 18 and 19.

1. What incidents show that Saul felt threatened by David?
2. In what ways did Saul try to cope with that threat?
3. How did Saul's own family help David?
4. What evidence do you see that God was protecting David?
5. When and where do you need God's protection today? Ask Him for it.

3

WHAT MAKES A GOOD FRIEND?

1 Samuel 20

Friendship. For some of us, friendships—some casual, some deep—bring meaning to life. Without friends life would be stale, dull, predictable. In addition, we depend on friends to help us verify our self-worth. We say, "Sara likes me; she's my friend—I must be worth something."

But others shy away from friendships. Perhaps they were once burned by a false friend. Or they had a friendship that became too demanding and the losses outweighed the gains. Or they prefer privacy and therefore close out the inner person to all outsiders.

As we study David, we encounter his friendship with Jonathan. From it we can discover what makes a God-centered friendship. And we can take a hard look at some of those gains and losses.

Helps for leaders can be found at the back of the book.

Read aloud 1 Samuel 18:1–9 and all of chapter 20.

1. What phrases in this passage help define the friendship between David and Jonathan? (Mention verses where you find these.) _____

_____

_____

_____

_____

2. What are some of the ingredients of that friendship?

_____

_____

3. What barriers existed to this friendship?

_____

_____

_____

How did David and Jonathan overcome these differences? _____

_____

_____

_____

_____

4. What steps did Jonathan take to communicate Saul's plans to David? _____

_____

_____

_____

5. What did David and Jonathan promise each other?

_____

_____

_____

6. What risks did their friendship bring to each of these men? _____

_____

_____

_____

7. What value might each person have found in the friendship? (Think of political, emotional, spiritual values.) _____

_____

_____

_____

8. What indication is there that they placed their friendship under God's rule? _____

_____

_____

9. What effects might submitting a friendship to God's control have on that relationship? _____

_____

_____

_____

_____

_____

10. Some people hesitate to form intense friendships because of the risks involved. What would you expect to gain and what would you expect to give up in an intense friendship? _____

_____

_____

_____

11. What counsel would you offer a person who felt alone, as if he needed a Jonathan, but had never found one?

_____

_____

_____

THROUGH THE WEEK

Day 1
Read Psalm 11.

1. What reasons does David have for being afraid?
2. Why can David feel confident even though he must "flee like a bird"?
3. In what ways will the wicked and upright fare differently under the Lord's examination?
4. What would it mean to you to see the face of the righteous Lord?
5. Talk to God today about some of the fears that make you want to run away. Let Him be your refuge.

Day 2
Read Psalm 59.

1. Try to see in your mind the images David paints. What do these images convey of David's feelings about his enemies?
2. What is David asking God to do and not do?
3. What purpose does he give God's actions?
4. What is David's response to God?
5. Choose a hymn that praises a quality in God that you value. Sing it as your morning prayer to Him.

Day 3
Read 1 Samuel 21:1–22:5.

1. What events in this passage seem unlikely for a man anointed to be king?
2. In what ways did David practice deceit here?
3. What risk did David place on Ahimelech?
4. Why was David's flight to Gath unsuccessful?

5. What composes David's "kingdom" by the end of this passage?
6. Do you think God approved of David's methods here? Why, or why not?

Day 4
Read Psalm 34.

1. What words and phrases indicate the kind of leader David intends to be?
2. What surprising instructions do you find from someone who appears to need a military victory?
3. How does David draw on his own experience in order to call others to God?
4. What does David reveal about the nature of the God he serves?
5. What do you find appealing about David's invitation to know God?
6. Which of these characteristics of God is close enough to your own experience that you might say to others,

   "Glorify the LORD with me; let us exalt his name together"?

7. Try to spend some time today exalting God's name with one other person.

Day 5
Read Psalm 56.

1. How does David characterize his enemies?
2. When have you felt in a similar position?
3. What does David expect God to do?
4. What reasons does David give why God might help him?
5. What does it mean to "trust" (verses 3, 4, and 11)?
6. How are fear and trust related?

7. When you are afraid, what practical difference can trust in God make?
8. How can you increase your trust in God at such a time?

Day 6
Read Psalm 52.

1. Find as many expressions as you can of David's anger.
2. In what sense does he see this as also God's anger?
3. For an explanation of this wrath, see 1 Samuel 21:7 and 22:6–23.
4. In what sense does Saul and his head shepherd, Doeg, deserve the indictment of Psalm 52:1–7?
5. Why might David also be thinking of himself as he writes these verses?
6. In what respect does David see his standing with God unchanged in spite of this disaster?
7. Bring to mind one event when you have been less than you should for God. Thank God now for His "unfailing love" in spite of that occurrence.

4

REVENGE OR RECONCILIATION?

1 Samuel 23–24

The situation for David had worsened. Three times Saul in a fit of temper had hurled a spear at him. Even Jonathan had to admit that David's life was in danger.

So David ran, first to Ahimelech, a priest at Nob, for provisions and a weapon, then to Gath, a bordering kingdom. But in Gath, the king's servants recognized David, forcing him to pretend insanity. This prompted King Achish to complain, "Am I so short of madmen that you have to bring this fellow here?"

So David escaped from Gath and hid out in a cave with some four hundred renegades. Later he returned to Judah as a fugitive, only to discover that Saul had killed eighty-five priests at Nob and murdered even the children of the town as a punishment for Ahimelech's helping David escape.

Then Saul came after David. And David ran, hoping to avoid confrontation. But should they meet, David had every reason to seek revenge.

Helps for leaders can be found at the back of the book.

*1. From what you know thus far of David, how would you describe his feelings toward Saul? _____

_____

*How would you expect him to react if he met Saul face to face? _____

_____

Read silently 1 Samuel 23. (Look for continued steps in the conflict between Saul and David.)

2. What points of conflict do you see between these two men? _____

_____

_____

_____

3. In what particulars do you see God being active?

_____

_____

_____

4. What might David have found encouraging about the happenings in this account? _____

_____

_____

_____

Read aloud 1 Samuel 24.

5. When David saw Saul entering the cave, what different actions might he have taken? _____

_____

*optional question

_____

_____

_____

*What outcome might each of these actions have had?

_____

_____

_____

6. What arguments did David use to attempt reconciliation with Saul? _____

_____

_____

_____

7. In what sense did Saul accept David's words?

_____

_____

If you had been David, what more would you have liked to hear from Saul? _____

_____

*8. In a land where new kings customarily killed their rivals, why do you think David agreed to Saul's request?

_____

9. Given the story thus far, what would you guess to be the outcome of this agreement? _____

_____

10. Why might you sometimes not want to be reconciled with another person? _____

_____

_____

_____

11. What has to happen in a conflict situation before reconciliation can be genuine? _____

_____

_____

_____

12. If David knew Saul as well as we do, why do you think
he promised not to seek revenge, and even attempted
reconciliation? _____

_____

_____

13. What part does David's view of God play in this drama?

_____

_____

14. Think of one person who has wronged you. (No names
aloud please.) _____

If David's God is your Lord, how might your knowledge
of Him affect this relationship? _____

_____

_____

15. How might your relationship with God help you endure
the risk of reconciliation with that person?

_____

_____

THROUGH THE WEEK

Days 1 and 2
Read Psalms 140 and 142.

Answer these questions for each psalm.

1. What can you know of David's circumstances from this psalm?
2. What does David believe to be true about God?
3. What does this psalm reveal of David's relationship with God?
4. What does he ask God to do?
5. Find one characteristic of God that you value. Pray, praising Him for that quality.

Day 3
Read Psalm 86.

1. This psalm is a masterpiece of balance—much like a jeweler's scale with gems of exactly the same weight on both sides. Find as many points of balance as you can. (Look for the words: *for, but, and, that.*) Then look for ideas that balance.
2. What do the concepts on either side of these balance points suggest about David's worship?
3. Find as many lines of praise to God as you can.
4. Select one of these and meditate on it. Ask yourself, what does this characteristic of God mean? How is the world different because God is this way? When have I seen this quality displayed? What can I expect God to do because He is this kind of God?
5. Pray. Praise and worship God, emphasizing this particular characteristic.

Day 4
Read again Psalm 86.

1. What can you know of David's spiritual temperature from this psalm?
2. What can you know of his physical circumstances?
3. What value does he seem to place on each?
4. What promises does he make to God?
5. Read slowly verse 11. What areas of your life would be affected if you were to make this promise of God? What good would you expect to come from it?
6. If you are able to do so honestly, pray the words of verse 11.

Day 5
Read Psalm 26.

1. Imagine David as the wronged person in a legal dispute where God will be the judge. What is his attitude toward God, the judge?
2. Why is he able to invite God to, "Try me"?
3. How might David's view of God as judge affect his actions toward King Saul?
4. What do you know about God that could help you say, even under stress, "My feet stand on level ground"?
5. Pray, thanking God for that.

Day 6
Read Psalm 57.

1. Read this psalm aloud, letting your mind see the word pictures that David paints.
2. What is your emotional response to this painting?
3. Which words and phrases give you a sense of God's immensity?

4. What contrast does David see between his own condition and the God he worships?
5. At what points do David and his God touch one another?
6. What difference does it make to you that you worship a God whose "love reaches to the heavens" and whose "faithfulness reaches to the skies"?

5

WHO WAS DAVID'S GOD?

Psalm 62

You've just finished one quarter of your study of David. You have begun to know the man David: what he does, what he thinks, how he prays.

But what makes David the person that he is? Why does he behave the way he does? Why can he exert all of his energy fleeing from Saul, yet when the opportunity arises to rid himself of this enemy, he spares Saul's life? To answer these questions, we must know David's God.

And David himself introduces us to God in his prayer of Psalm 62.

Read aloud Psalm 62.

1. How does this psalm make you feel?

_____

2. Find as many words as you can that reveal who God is and what He is like. _____
_____

Helps for leaders can be found at the back of the book.

_____

_____

_____

3. What do you think David means when he says that God is a *rock* and a *fortress*? (Try forming mental pictures to help you define these words.) _____

_____

_____

What do the words *refuge* and *salvation* add to this picture of God's character? _____

_____

_____

4. Why would these qualities be of value to David?

_____

_____

5. Share with the group a time when you have experienced God being a rock, a fortress, or a refuge.

_____

_____

6. What words and phrases does David use to describe people? _____

_____

7. If you believed this to be true of people (including your-self) how might your expectations change?

_____

_____

8. What else does David point to that people sometimes trust instead of God? _____

_____

9. Why might some people prefer to trust the "things" of verses 9 and 10 rather than God? _____

_____

_____

10. Several times David uses the term "God alone." In what sense is God more worthy of trust than anything else David cites in this psalm? (Contrast the qualities of God with the qualities of: people, verses 3–4; prestige, verse 9; power, verse 10; and money, verse 10.)

_____

_____

_____

11. Look again at verses 11 and 12. Of what value is it to you that your God is both strong and loving?

_____

_____

12. What does it mean to you that you can "pour out your heart" (verse 8) to this kind of God? _____

_____

_____

13. Spend a few moments thinking silently about this psalm. What do you value in it? _____

_____

_____

THROUGH THE WEEK

Days 1 through 5
Read slowly one of these psalms each day: Psalm 17, 54, 143, 64, 70. Then note answers from each psalm for the following questions.

1. What reasons does this psalm give for David's refusal to harm Saul?
2. What words and phrases show that David takes a realistic view of his harsh circumstances?
3. What qualities in God lead David to worship?
4. What does David see as important about the way he conducts his life?
5. Review the spiritual goals David expresses in this psalm. Which of these goals would you like to adopt?

   Talk to God about it.

Day 6
Read Psalm 133.

1. What word pictures describe the unity of God's people?
2. What indication is there that unity between God's people is of great value?
3. What steps has David taken thus far to preserve unity among the people of God?
4. What steps could you take to protect the unity that God has created between you and fellow believers?

6

CAN I CREATE PEACE?

1 Samuel 25

Shrieks carom off the walls of the bedroom shared by your six-year-old twin boys. A new dump truck, original object of the brawl, lies forgotten in the corner as the twins roll over and over, kicking and pummeling each other with any free extremity. You . . .

The annual church business meeting is three hours old. For the last hour, the congregation has debated whether church members should receive payment for serving the church. Should you pay the organist but not the janitor? Should you pay the organist and janitor but not a Sunday school teacher? Tempers are frayed. Feelings are hurt. Children are fussy. You . . .

Your husband hasn't spoken to you for a week. If you speak to him he glares at you and walks out of the room. You . . .

Hostile situations. Some small, some mountainous. We bump into them daily. Can we make peace? Should we? How?

Helps for leaders can be found at the back of the book.

Read aloud 1 Samuel 25.

1. How would you describe the character of each major person in this drama? _____

_____

_____

_____

_____

_____

_____

2. What did David want from Nabal? _____

_____

3. How did Nabal's servants differ from Nabal in their views of this request? _____

_____

_____

_____

4. Once David and his men were on the march, what options were open to Abigail? _____

_____

_____

_____

What would have happened if Abigail had followed each of these routes? _____

_____

_____

5. Take a hard look at the way you deal with hostile situations. If you had just learned that David and his four hundred men were marching your direction, what would you have done? _____

   _____

6. What details show that Abigail was willing to expend a lot of effort in order to make peace? _____

   _____

   _____

7. List the arguments Abigail used to convince David not to follow his plan of vengeance. _____

   _____

   _____

   _____

   _____

   _____

8. What insights did Abigail show into David's character, his future, and his God? _____

   _____

   _____

   _____

   _____

9. In what ways did Abigail's efforts for peace reflect sensitivity to the people around her? (Consider her actions toward the servants, Nabal, and David.)

   _____

   _____

10. How did David and Abigail's view of God enable David to say in verse 35, "Go home in peace"?

_____

_____

_____

_____

11. In what ways did God provide for the short-term and long-term needs of both David and Abigail?

_____

_____

_____

_____

12. What do you know about God that might cause you to work for peace when you'd rather take revenge or run from the conflict? _____

_____

_____

_____

_____

13. What has to happen in a hostile situation in order for peace to be genuine? _____

_____

_____

_____

_____

14. Think of one hostile situation where there is a possibility that you could make peace. Without detailing the background, what concrete step could you take toward a peaceful solution? _____

_____

_____

_____

_____

_____

THROUGH THE WEEK

Day 1
Read Psalm 101.

1. Find as many promises as you can in this psalm.
2. If David were to follow these promises that he makes to God, what effect would they have on his marriage?
3. How might his family (wives, children, servants) benefit by his keeping these promises?
4. What effect would his household have on the surrounding community? (Note: Some of these actions would be carried out in David's role as king, not just as husband.)
5. Mentally review the activities and relationships within your own family. If you were to follow David's vow of verse 2 and walk in your house with blameless heart, what major change would you need to make?

   Are you willing to make this change with God's help? Bring it to Him in prayer.

Day 2
Read 1 Samuel 26.

1. In what ways is this event similar to the one in 1 Samuel 24? How is it different?
2. Why might David have even more reason to kill Saul this time?
3. What experiences recorded in chapter 25 might have helped David speak as he did to Abishai?
4. What is David's principle reason for not attacking Saul?
5. What reasons did David give Saul not to pursue him any longer?
6. Think of one person with whom you believe that God expects you to be unusually lenient. Ask that He give you His own patient endurance.

Day 3
Read 1 Samuel 27.

1. What did David do to protect himself from Saul?
2. What do you find distasteful about David's behavior in Ziklag?

   Note: The people David raided here were enemies of both Achish and Israel. (Review 1 Samuel 15.)
3. What steps was David forced to take once he began to deceive Achish?
4. When have you begun a small deception and found it much larger than you intended?

   If you are ready, confess this to God and ask His help now in untangling yourself from its results.

Day 4
Read Psalm 7.

1. If you had been David at Ziklag, why might you think this a dangerous prayer to pray?
2. David quotes three proverbs in verses 14–16. If these proverbs are true, what do you think might happen next at Ziklag?
3. Why might you hesitate to say to God,

   "Judge me, O Lord, according to my righteousness, according to my integrity, O Most High, O righteous God, who searches minds and hearts"?

4. Meditate on the righteousness of Jesus Christ.
5. Have you accepted Christ's righteousness as a substitute for your own and given yourself to Jesus as your Lord? If so, thank God for this gift. Then pray, keeping in mind that you do not need to approach God on the basis of your own goodness, but through Jesus Christ.

Day 5
Read God's command to his people
   in Deuteronomy 18:9–13.
Now read 1 Samuel 28.

1. If you were creating a painting based on this event, what would you include in your painting? What colors would you choose?
2. In what ways does Saul appear less than a king in this account?
3. Why do you think he was so desperate to talk with Samuel?
4. Review 1 Samuel 15:26–29. Why is Saul now more likely to believe Samuel's similar words of 28:16–19?
5. What effect might this picture of a man abandoned by God have on your own relationship with God?

Day 6
Read 1 Samuel 29 and 30.

1. What do you think David would have done if the Philistine commanders had not objected to his presence?
2. What reasons did you have to suspect that David's absence might promote a raid on Ziklag? (Review 1 Samuel 27:8–11 and Psalm 7:14–16.)
3. What evidence do you see that David still depended on God for strength and guidance?
4. What reasons did David give for the way he divided the spoils of battle?
5. What does God's continued presence with David, in spite of his shortcomings, suggest about God's relationship with His people?

   Spend some time thanking God for this quality in Himself.

7

DO I TRY TO PLAY GOD?

1 Samuel 31–2 Samuel 2:7

Do you try to play God?

"Of course not," you reply, "I know my place. And be-sides, what little I know of God shows me I'm not up to His job."

But think again. Do you observe another person, perhaps a person in your family, and try to manipulate that person into the shape you think he or she should become?

Do you set a goal for yourself, maybe one that you believe is God's will, then march toward it purposely closing your eyes to people you might brush aside in your wake?

Do you view someone else's actions through narrowed eyes and say, "I know that's sin," and thereafter purposely avoid that person?

A fine line stands between using our God-given abilities to bring structure to our lives and rushing ahead trying to do what only God should do.

Helps for leaders can be found at the back of the book.

David looked at that line. At times he may have stepped over it. But in at least one area, David stepped back and let God do the job.

Read aloud 1 Samuel 31.

1. According to this passage, exactly how did Saul die?

_____

_____

_____

2. What actions show the degree of Israelite defeat?

_____

_____

_____

3. What incidents led to David's being absent when Saul was killed? _____

_____

_____

_____

Why might David be grateful that he was not present?

_____

_____

*4. What national and personal losses did David suffer because of this battle? _____

_____

_____

_____

_____
*optional question

_____

_____

5. How would you expect David to respond to news of Saul's death? _____

_____

Read aloud 2 Samuel 1:1–16.

6. In what ways did the Amalekite messenger's account of Saul's death differ from the story in the previous chapter? _____

_____

_____

Why do you think the Amalekite told the story differently? _____

_____

7. Why did David order the messenger's execution?

_____

Read aloud 2 Samuel 1:17–2:7.

8. In what sense do David's words in the lament about Saul and Jonathan reflect a broader picture than his own point of view? _____

_____

_____

_____

*9. Why do you think the writer tells of this anointing in such a terse way? _____

_____

_____

_____

_____

10. Ever since Samuel anointed him, David had known that
    God would someday make him king. At what points in
    his life might he have been tempted to take matters into
    his own hands and hurry the process?

    _____

    _____

    _____

    Why might he be glad now that he had waited and let
    God bring about the kingship in His own time?

    _____

    _____

11. What kinds of things ought we to stand back from and
    let God do? _____

    _____

    _____

12. What are you waiting for now that only God can do?

    _____

    When are you tempted to play God and try to do the job
    for Him? _____

    _____

    How might David's experience help you while you
    wait? _____

    _____

THROUGH THE WEEK

Day 1
Read Psalm 40.

1. What advantage does David see to waiting?
2. What does David thank God for? (See verses 1–5.)
3. What does he promise God? (See verses 6–10.)
4. What does he ask of God? (See verses 11–16.)
5. If this prayer had been written by your king, what would you value in him?
6. Think of one setting where you must lead (home, church, club, school, work). Which of the qualities expressed here would you like to claim as your own?

Day 2
Read Psalm 21.

1. In what way does David believe that he became king?
2. What does David say that God has done? (Find all that you can.)
3. What does he expect God to yet do?
4. Why might David's review of God's past actions help him as he thinks of the future?
5. How might this psalm help you as you wait for God to work?

Day 3
Read Psalm 144.

1. If this psalm were a mirror, what would David see in himself? (See especially verses 1–4, 7–10, 15.)
2. If the mirror were next turned to God, what would David see in God?

3. Which requests in this prayer might David make in his new role as king?
4. How might this psalm serve as an antidote for excessive pride?
5. Meditate on verses 1–4.
   Talk to God about some of your thoughts.

Day 4
Read Psalm 61.

1. In what different ways does David acknowledge that he depends on God?
2. In what sense does David give himself to God?
3. What do you depend on God for?
4. What other needs ought you to turn over to Him? If you are able, do so now.

Day 5
Read 2 Samuel 2, 3, 4, and 5.

1. Draw a chart of steps. On the bottom step write "David is annointed king of Judah (2:4)." On the top step write, "David, king of Judah and Israel, conquers Jerusalem (5:7)." On the intervening steps, note significant happenings between these two events.
2. What acts of violence in these chapters do you find morally offensive?
3. What instances do you see of David trying to play fair, even in war?
4. Where do you wish he had acted differently?
5. Read again 1 Samuel 16:1. The chapters from 1 Samuel 16 through 2 Samuel 5 account for many years of David's life. What does this passage of time and the intervening events tell you about God's care for his people?

Day 6
Read Psalm 65.

1. Note the many works of God in this praise psalm.
2. Now write your own psalm of praise using the actions of God that are particularly significant to you. You might begin as David did:

   Praise awaits you, O God, of _____;
   to you my vows will be fulfilled.   (your name)
   O you who . . .

3. When you are finished writing, read your prayer of praise to God.

8

SHOULD I FEAR GOD?

2 Samuel 6

At Saul's death, David was anointed king of Judah. Meanwhile, Ish-Bosheth, Saul's son, remained king over the rest of Israel. After a series of battles, David's forces grew stronger while Ish-Bosheth's diminished. Attempts were made to unite the two factions peacefully, but treachery and murder interrupted the delicate negotiations. Then Ish-Bosheth was killed in his bed by his own soldiers.

Now without a leader, all of Israel joined David's side. David made a compact with them before the Lord at Hebron, and they anointed him king of all Israel. Soon after, David captured the fortress city of Jerusalem. Hiram, king of Tyre, built David a palace there. At this point, David decided to bring the Ark of God into Jerusalem. (Summary of 2 Samuel 2–5.)

Helps for leaders can be found at the back of the book.

Read aloud 2 Samuel 6:1–11.

1. What preparations did David make for bringing the ark of God to Jerusalem? (Use only verses 1–5.)

_____

_____

_____

_____

Note: The ark of God was a rectangular box made of acacia wood, and measured 4 x 2½ x 2½ feet. The whole was covered with gold and was carried on poles inserted in rings at the four lower corners. The lid, or 'mercy-seat,' was a gold plate surrounded by two cherubs with outspread wings.

The ark held two tablets recording the Ten Commandments and also a pot of manna and Aaron's rod. The ark was made at Sinai by Bezaleel to the pattern given to Moses. (*New Bible Dictionary*, page 82.)

2. What went wrong on this first attempt to bring back the ark? _____

_____

_____

3. What were David's reactions to Uzzah's death?

_____

_____

_____

4. Why do you think Uzzah died? _____

_____

_____

5. Read Numbers 4:15 and 1 Chronicles 15:11–15. What do these verses add to your ideas about Uzzah's death?

   _____

   _____

   What do they emphasize about the nature of God?

   _____

   _____

6. How do you feel about this aspect of God's nature?

   _____

   _____

Read aloud 2 Samuel 6:12–23.

7. Why did David try once again to bring the ark to Jerusalem? _____

   _____

   _____

8. When David moved the ark this time, what did he do differently? _____

   _____

   _____

   Why? _____

   _____

*9. Why do you think Michal responded as she did? (For a survey of Michal's past, review 1 Samuel 18:20–21; 19:11–17; 25:42–44; 2 Samuel 3:13–16.)

_____

*optional question

_____

_____

_____

*10. What do you think caused David to react to Michal the
way he did? _____

_____

11. What ingredients of worship do you find in bringing the
ark to Jerusalem? _____

_____

_____

_____

_____

12. What are we saying about God if we try to worship Him
but are lax about obeying Him? _____

_____

_____

To what extent do you think our worship of God should
include fear? _____

_____

_____

13. When are you tempted to reword a command of God's
so that it is easier to obey? _____

_____

_____

_____

_____

14. How might an appropriate fear of God help you deal with that temptation? _____

_____

_____

_____

_____

_____

THROUGH THE WEEK

This week study Psalms 15, 24, 27, 30, 68, and 138. Each of these psalms is a hymn of praise designed for group worship. Their words have been incorporated into numerous songs and hymns. Plan for your week of study by locating each psalm (or a part of it) in a folk psalter, songbook of rhymed psalms, or traditional hymnal. (Many such books index hymns with appropriate Scripture.) Then, as part of your daily worship, sing or read a song based on the psalm you have studied. Do this as a prayer of worship.

Days 1–6
Read one of the above psalms each day, noting answers to the following questions.

1. What does David value in God's character? (Find as much as you can.)
2. Which of these qualities is special to you? Why?
3. Thank and praise God for that quality, remembering any occasion when you saw that particular characteristic displayed.
4. What does David say is an appropriate response to this kind of God?

   Worship involves our whole self as we respond to God's whole person. Sometime this week, try a creative form of worship relating to a phrase from one of these psalms. Sing, draw a sketch, paint, write a poem or descriptive paragraph, dance to a song of praise. Offer this activity as worship.

9

WHO PLANS MY LIFE?

2 Samuel 7

Who plans your life?

"I do," the quick reply—perhaps a little defensive.

Or a belligerent, "My husband and kids, plus the PTA and church Christian Education Council, not to mention the little man who sits inside my telephone and rings it all day long."

Or a constricted, "I think my parents did; everything I do seems to hark back to those early days. Maybe it's in my genes."

Who planned David's life? At one point, David answered quickly, "I do." Then something happened to change his mind.

Read aloud 2 Samuel 7:1–17.

1. What prompted David to plan a house for the ark of God?

Helps for leaders can be found at the back of the book.

_____

_____

_____

2. How did God describe His relationship in the past with the nation of Israel? (See verses 6–7.)

_____

_____

_____

With David? (See verses 8–9.) _____

_____

_____

3. What do you think God was trying to tell David through this recounting of history? _____

_____

_____

_____

4. What did God promise the nation of Israel?

_____

_____

_____

What did He promise David personally?

_____

_____

_____

_____

*5. What did God mean when He told David, "I will establish the throne of his kingdom forever" (v. 13)? See also Luke 2:4–11. _____

_____

*What effect does this promise of David have on you?

_____

6. How did David's plan and God's plan differ?

_____

_____

7. How do you think Nathan felt about bringing this message from God to David? _____

_____

_____

8. What evidence have you seen that God is designing a pattern for your life? _____

_____

_____

_____

Read aloud 2 Samuel 7:18–29.

9. What words and phrases help define David's relationship with God? _____

_____

_____

_____

_____

_____

*optional question

10. What emotions did this relationship evoke in David?

    _____

    _____

11. How did David describe the relationship between God and Israel? (See verses 23–24.) _____

    _____

    _____

    _____

    In what way might a Hebrew who was less aware of God have viewed this relationship differently?

    _____

    _____

    _____

12. In his prayer, David addresses God many times as "O Sovereign Lord." How does his prayer help define what he means by *sovereign*? _____

    _____

    _____

    _____

    _____

13. Look again at verse 28. What events in your life have helped you believe that God's purposes for you are good? _____

    _____

    _____

    _____

THROUGH THE WEEK

Day 1
Read Psalm 16.

1. What comparisons does David draw between his God and other gods? (See verses 1–4.)
2. What phrases show that David believes God has planned his life?
3. How does David feel about those plans?
4. How might David's words help you cope with a reluctance to let Someone other than yourself hold the reins of your life?
5. Spend a few moments mentally reviewing the stages of your past.
   Thank God for those points where you can now see that He nudged you toward a good path.

Day 2
Read Psalm 145.

1. David says in verse 3 that no one can fathom God's greatness. What phrases does he use as he attempts to describe the greatness of God?
2. What indications do you find that God's greatness is available to a wide variety of people?
3. If David were thinking of his own children when he wrote verse 4, what mighty acts do you think he would tell them about?
4. What acts of God in your life would you like to recount to your children?
5. Try to spend some time today commending God's works to someone of another generation.

Day 3
Read Psalm 103.

1. In verse 2, David says we should "forget not all God's benefits." What benefits does David remind us of? (See verses 3–10.)

2. How does David define God's love (verses 11–14)?

3. What contrasts does David draw between people and God in verses 15–19?

4. What effects does David see his own relationship with God having on his children?

5. In what context does David visualize his praise (see verses 20–22)?

6. How might an awareness that your own worship joins that of the angels, heavenly hosts, and God's own work affect your praise of God?

7. Make a brief list of what you can praise God for. (Include some of David's ideas if you like.) Pray from this list, praising God.

Day 4
Read 2 Samuel chapters 8, 9, and 10.

1. What do these chapters add to your view of David's character?

2. What do you appreciate and what do you dislike?

3. What indication is there that David's victories were not due entirely to his own military power?

4. Review David's promise to Jonathan in 1 Samuel 20:14–17 and the introduction to Mephibosheth in 2 Samuel 4:4. What steps did David take to keep that promise?

5. When have you wished you could repay a kindness but been unable to do so?

6. Kindness need not be repaid to the same person. (Jonathan

was dead and David could not repay him personally.) Today, remember a time when someone was kind to you and repay that kindness to someone else.

Day 5
Read Psalm 60.

David did not win all his battles. He wrote Psalm 60 after an embarrassing defeat.

1. What does David believe is the reason he lost the battle?
2. How does David view the land and cities around him?
3. What hope does he have for the future?
4. When have you felt that you lost a battle?
5. How might an earnest belief that, win or lose, the territory belongs to God help you at a time like that?

Day 6
Read Psalm 18.

1. How is David's description of his circumstances at the beginning of this psalm different than the description of his later circumstances?
2. How did this change come about?
3. How does David account for his military success?
4. What dangers might arise from the attitude expressed in verses 20–24?
5. Read again verses 1, 3–6, 19. What steps are you taking to become the kind of person that God delights in?
6. How could knowing that God delights in you affect your view of yourself?

10

DOES MY SIN MATTER TO GOD?

2 Samuel 11–12

When it comes to sin, we're full of excuses. We say:

—It's the only way to get ahead in business.
—It's a small sin.
—The other person did it to me first; I'm only dishing out what he deserves.
—It's a hidden sin; no one knows about it but me.
—The end justifies the means.
—Everybody does it.
—It doesn't hurt anybody.
—God knows I'm human.

But in spite of all this logic, sin still nags at our minds. Instead of looking inward and trying to defend ourselves, let's look up for a moment and ask, "Does my sin matter to God?"

Helps for leaders can be found at the back of the book.

Read aloud 2 Samuel 11.

1. What emotions do you find in this story?

   _____

   _____

2. What steps did David take in attempting to solve the problem of Bathsheba's pregnancy? _____

   _____

   _____

   _____

3. What can you know of Uriah from this account?

   _____

   _____

   _____

*4. What hints do you find that David should not have been at home in Jerusalem during the time of this incident? (See also 2 Samuel 12:26–28.) _____

   _____

   _____

*5. Why might you suspect that Joab was not entirely trustworthy? _____

   _____

Read aloud 2 Samuel 12.

6. How were these circumstances of Nathan's coming different than the last time God sent him to David? (Glance back at 2 Samuel 7.) _____

---

*optional question

_____

_____

7. Why do you think Nathan began with a parable?

_____

_____

8. What did the characters in Nathan's parable symbolize?

_____

9. What reasons did God give for why David should not have behaved with Bathsheba as he did?

_____

_____

_____

_____

10. What did God say would be the result of David's sin?

_____

_____

*Do you feel that the promised punishment fit the crime? _____

*Why, or why not? _____

_____

11. Examine carefully David's words, "I have sinned against the Lord" (verse 13). What ingredients of repentance are contained here? _____

_____

_____

_____

_____

_____

12. Why do you think God punished David if He had already forgiven him? _____

_____

_____

13. Why did David's servants have trouble understanding their master's behavior during his child's sickness and death? _____

_____

14. What can you find to admire in David? (Survey the whole chapter.) _____

_____

_____

_____

15. When are you tempted to treat sin more casually than you should? _____

_____

16. What could you remember from these chapters that might help you resist sin? _____

_____

_____

_____

_____

THROUGH THE WEEK

Day 1
Read Psalm 22.

1. Read this psalm twice. First pick out phrases that could relate to David's suffering over his own sin. Read the psalm a second time noting phrases that might refer to Christ's suffering for all our sins.
2. What does this psalm reveal to be the nature of suffering? (Look at physical effects, emotional effects, effects on relationships.)
3. Look again at verses 1 and 2. What do verses 3–5 suggest as an example for prayer when we feel that God is far away?
4. What do verses 19–21 add to the kind of praying we might do at such a time?
5. Why would the hope found in verses 22–31 be hard to verbalize under these circumstances?
6. How could this prayer motivate you to pray even if you felt a great gulf between you and God?

Day 2*
Read Psalm 51.

1. When David brings his sin before the Lord, what does he ask God to do?
2. How does David's sin affect his relationship with God?
3. In what ways does he expect God to heal him?
4. How will David demonstrate his restored (renewed) relationship with God?

---

*This material is reprinted from Let's Pray Together, by Margaret Fromer and Sharrel Keyes (Wheaton, Ill.: Harold Shaw Publishers, 1974), p. 30. Used by permission.

5. In what areas of your life does God wish (right now) to cleanse, heal, and restore you to a joyful relationship with Himself?
6. Using this prayer as a model, ask God to come into your life to forgive and renew in the specific areas you mentioned.
7. What do you look forward to being able to do because you have been made whole?

Days 3, 4, and 5*

Divide your life into three (not necessarily equal) segments. For instance, childhood, teens, adulthood; or childhood through high school years, early adulthood, later adulthood.

Starting with the most *recent* period today and, working backward for the next three days, bring before God as specifically as possible the person that you were during those years. Because God *was* and *is* and *is to be*, you can invite Him to enter your past, and your memories or pictures of it, and cleanse and heal, forgive and put to rest any part of you that is in discord.

Pray the prayer of Psalm 51 as it is appropriate to each of these periods of your life.

Day 6
Read Psalm 6.

1. How does David illustrate the intensity of his sorrow?
2. What does he want God to do?
3. What reasons does he give God for doing this?
4. How does David express confidence in God?
5. Read aloud verse 9. Think back over our confessions to God during the past three days. Read this sentence as an affirmation of God's response to your prayers.

11

DOES CONFESSION HAVE HEALING POWER?

Psalm 32

What does guilt feel like?

A man shuffles through his day, head lowered, unable to look anyone in the eye.

A woman feels a nebulous unease. She can't put her finger on specific sin, but she's certain that it's there. She wears an anxious expression, never quite sure she's doing the right thing.

A teenager's life-of-the-party antics cover up his feeling of guilt. "Even God can't love me," he's certain. "But maybe if everyone has a good time because of me, someone will like me—and I won't feel quite so bad."

An old man bows his head to pray. But the words won't come. Guilt.

Guilt can tie us in knots. But God never meant us to live that way. He offers a solution.

Helps for leaders can be found at the back of the book.

Read aloud Psalm 32.

1. According to this psalm, what effects might unconfessed sin have? _____

   _____

   _____

   _____

2. Why might a person who has sinned want to keep silent—even to God? _____

   _____

   _____

3. What are the effects in your own life when you don't acknowledge sin? _____

   _____

   _____

   _____

4. What ingredients of repentance do you find here?

   _____

   _____

   _____

   _____

5. What is the difference between our covering our sin (v. 5) and God's covering it (v. 1)? _____

   _____

   _____

   _____

   _____

6. What qualities in God's character does this psalm reveal that might help you want to repent? _____

_____

_____

_____

7. How was David's life different after he had been forgiven? _____

_____

_____

8. What new demands were placed on David because of his repentance? (Review also Psalm 51:13–15.)

_____

_____

_____

_____

9. Why might this new relationship be both comforting and unsettling? _____

_____

_____

10. Under what circumstances have you experienced the sense of cleansing that verses 1, 2, and 11 describe?

_____

_____

_____

_____

11. Why are the words of verse 11 an appropriate aftermath to repentance? _____._____

_____

_____

12. What changes have occurred in your life after you have been forgiven? _____

_____

_____

_____

13. What steps in your own spiritual growth would you like to see as a result of your experience with the sequence of sin, repentance, forgiveness? _____

_____

_____

_____

THROUGH THE WEEK

Day 1
Read again Psalm 103.

1. What reassurance can you find in this psalm that God can and does forgive? (See verses 3–4, 8–10, and 12–14.)
2. Using the imagery in this psalm, how would you describe God's forgiveness?
3. If you have confessed your sin to God, you can claim this forgiveness as your own. Knowing this, how do you feel about your past? Your future?
4. Notice the beginning and ending of this psalm. Why is praise an appropriate response to God's forgiveness? Praise God in prayer today.

Day 2
Read 2 Samuel 13.

1. What indication do you see that Amnon did not rape his half sister, Tamar, on mere impulse?
2. What words and actions suggest the degree of damage done to Tamar?
3. Notice the time intervals in this chapter. How does the passing of time effect the emotions of the characters?
4. What part does lying and deceit play in this family tragedy?
5. What similarities do you see between the actions of David's sons and David's own sin with Bathsheba?
6. What does this suggest about the effect that our sins, even our forgiven sins, have on our children?
7. Pray today for your children, or for some other person under your influence. Ask that God protect them from your own shortcomings. Ask His help in living a godly example before them.

Day 3
Read Psalm 28.

1. What is David's mood as he writes this psalm?
2. What is his attitude toward those who deceive and harbor grudges?
3. What does David see as a cause of these sins?
4. How does David's prayer reflect a shepherd-like concern for his people?
5. For whom ought you to pray that God will be their shepherd? Do so.

Day 4
Read Psalm 5.

1. Find as many references as you can to uses of the tongue.
2. How does David describe God's response to sins of the tongue?
3. How does this differ from God's relationship with those who use their tongues in God-pleasing ways?
4. Spend some time now thinking about the ways you use your tongue. Confess to God those patterns of speech that spell rebellion against Him. Thank God for the gift of speech. Plan some time today to use your tongue in a way that pleases God.
5. Read verse 6 again. If this is true of Absalom, what pattern would you expect his life to take?

Day 5
Read 2 Samuel 14.

1. What instances do you see of people manipulating each other in order to get what they want?
2. Why did Joab ask the woman from Tekoa to concoct a story for David?
3. To what extent did David allow himself to be manipulated by this story? In what respect was he *not* deceived?

4. What techniques did Absalom use to get what he wanted.
5. How does David seem less a king than he did in previous chapters?
6. Judging by what you have seen so far, what would you expect to happen if Absalom gains in power?

Day 6
Read Psalm 12.

1. What phrases reveal the way David feels about his current circumstances?
2. What forms of lying does he condemn?
3. What comparison does he draw between God's words and the words of the people around him?
4. Why does he feel that God may act on his behalf?
5. Read again verse 6. Do you believe this is an accurate picture of God's words? If so, how ought this to affect the way you see Scripture?

12

WHERE IS GOD
WHEN MY WORLD CAVES IN?

2 Samuel 15–16

David's world had begun to crumble; it began in his own family. His oldest son, Amnon, tricked and then raped Tamar, a half sister. Tamar's full brother and David's third son, Absalom, then plotted revenge—and got it. Two years later, Absalom organized a party, got Amnon drunk, then ordered him killed.

Because of this, Absalom spent three years in exile. At the end of this period, Joab, David's chief military commander, manipulated David into allowing Absalom to return to Jerusalem. But for two more years, David refused to see his son. Eventually, Absalom bullied Joab (Absalom set Joab's fields on fire) into convincing David to see him. So seven years after he'd raped his sister, Absalom stood in David's court. And David kissed him.

Helps for leaders can be found at the back of the book.

Read aloud 2 Samuel 15.

1. What steps did Absalom take to win the people to his side? (See verses 1–6.) _____

_____

_____

_____

2. What maneuvers did he make to gain political control? (See verses 7–12.) _____

_____

_____

_____

*3. What steps did David take to protect his people?

_____

_____

His property? _____

_____

The city of Jerusalem? _____

_____

4. What groundwork did David lay for a possible return to Jerusalem? _____

_____

_____

_____

5. Read again verses 25–26. Why might sending the ark back to Jerusalem have been a hard decision?

_____

*optional question

_____

_____

What do these statements say of David's view of God?

_____

_____

_____

6. Why might you be afraid to say the words of verse 26?

_____

What do our fears of this kind of commitment reveal
about our picture of God? _____

_____

_____

7. How would you evaluate David's political situation at
the end of chapter 15? _____

_____

Read aloud 2 Samuel 16.

8. What further indignities did David suffer in this chapter?

_____

_____

_____

9. Review Nathan's prophecy after David's sin with Bathsheba (2 Samuel 12:10–14). What specific events fulfilled that prophecy? _____

_____

_____

_____

_____

_____

*10. Why was Ahithophel important to both David and Absalom? _____

_____

11. What role do you expect Hushai to play in Jerusalem?

_____

12. What evidence do you see that David still believes that God is in control of his world? _____

_____

_____

13. Though David's faith remained firm, what events might have led him to believe that God had abandoned him?

_____

_____

_____

_____

14. Under what circumstances might you feel that your world had caved in? _____

_____

_____

How might David's view of God help you at a time like that? _____

_____

_____

THROUGH THE WEEK

Days 1–5
Read the following psalms, one each day, and answer the questions below: Psalm 55, 41, 63, 3, and 4.

1. What words does David use to describe his circumstances?
2. How does David feel about his current condition?
3. What example or instruction for dealing with hardship can you find in this psalm?
4. If you were facing a hard time in your life, what comfort could you find here?
5. Think for a moment, "What is the worst thing that could happen to me?" Picture yourself in the midst of that fearsome situation. How might you draw on this psalm at a time like that?

Day 6
Read 2 Samuel 17.

1. How did Ahithophel's advice differ from Hushai's?
2. If you were Absalom, which battle plan would you favor? Why?
3. How did Hushai reflect respect for David even while giving advice to Absalom?
4. What secret steps did Hushai take to protect David?
5. Read again David's prayer of 2 Samuel 15:31. How did God answer that prayer?
6. Think of one friend who, like Hushai, has been faithful to you through thick and thin. Spend some of today's prayer time praying for that friend and thanking God for him or her.

13

WHERE IS GOD WHEN I FALL APART?

2 Samuel 18–19:8

A crumbled world sometimes results in a crushed person. Each of us has a breaking point. For some, a plate of burnt toast will do it; for others it would take a holocaust to do them in. Most of us fall somewhere between. But inside, we have a secret prayer that says, "Oh God, don't let *that* happen—I couldn't take it."

But what happens when we do fall apart—either momentarily or massively. Where is God then?

Read aloud 2 Samuel 18–19:8.

1. What mental pictures do you see as you read this narrative? _____

_____

_____

_____

Helps for leaders can be found at the back of the book.

_____

_____

_____

What mood does each of these pictures create?

_____

2. What preparations did David make for the battle with Absalom? _____

_____

_____

3. Exactly how did Absalom die? _____

_____

_____

_____

_____

4. What underlying concerns did Joab, Ahimaaz, and the Cushite each have about the message that must be delivered to David? _____

_____

_____

_____

How did each of these men seem out of touch with David's feelings? _____

_____

_____

_____

_____

5. What can you know of David's state of mind as he waited for news of the battle? _____

_____

_____

_____

6. What arguments did Joab use in convincing David to stop mourning Absalom's death? _____

_____

_____

_____

_____

Why do you think David responded to Joab as he did?

_____

7. If you were a king, would you want Joab to be your top aid? _____

_____

Why, or why not? _____

_____

_____

_____

8. Briefly review 2 Samuel chapters 13–17 looking at Absalom's character. Why do you think God did not grant David's desire that he should die in Absalom's place (See 2 Samuel 18:33.) _____

_____

_____

9. What events in today's passage suggest that God still cared for David and his people? _____

_____

_____

_____

10. Page back over David's life and writings. What reasons might he have for hope even while he mourns for Absalom? _____

_____

_____

_____

11. As you continue to think over David's life and writings, what one incident or phrase might you latch on to in a time of personal despair? _____

_____

_____

_____

THROUGH THE WEEK

Day 1
Read 2 Samuel 19:9–21:22.

1. How did David exercise his power as judge in the following incidents: 2 Samuel 19:15–23; 19:24–30: 19:31–39?
2. Why do you think that David treated the ten concubines as he did? (See 2 Samuel 20:3. Review also 2 Samuel 16:21–22.)
3. How did friction begin between Judah and Israel? (See 19:9–15 and 19:40–20:2.)
4. What contrasts can you find in the way David treated Sheba's revolt (chapter 20) and the way he treated Absalom's revolt?
   Why do you think he treated them so differently?
5. Why do you think Joab killed Amasa the way he did?
   Note: Chapter 21 begins with the words "During the reign of David." The last four chapters of 2 Samuel function as an appendix to the book. They recount isolated events not previously recorded but fitting into some past period of his life.
6. What incidents in chapter 21 exhibit God's power?
7. How might you benefit from the account of David's history in these chapters?

Days 2, 3, and 4

For the next three days, you will read a series of imprecatory psalms, or the "psalms of cursing." If you have followed David's life this far, you are fully aware that David's actions were not always perfect—and neither is every psalm a perfect example of worship. These psalms, likely written after his flight from Absalom, represent a thoroughly human bitterness painted with the colorful imagery of a gifted poet. In order to see David's cursings in perspective, read the following Old Testament passages that deal with God's commands regarding our enemies: Leviticus 19:17–18; Exodus 23:4–5; Proverbs 24:17; 25:21.

Of these psalms of cursing, C.S. Lewis said:

> We must face [two] facts squarely. The hatred is there—festering, gloating, undisguised—and also we would be wicked if we in any way condoned or approved it, or (worse still) used it to justify similar passions in ourselves. Only after these two admissions have been made can we safely proceed. . . . The reaction of the Psalmists to injury, though profoundly natural, is profoundly wrong.
>
> —C.S. Lewis, pp. 22, 26

Study one psalm each day, using the following questions. Psalms 109, 58, 69.

1. What can you know of David's circumstances from this psalm?
2. What can you find in it that is right and good?
3. What phrases in this psalm go against the teachings cited above in Leviticus, Exodus, and Proverbs?
4. Spend some time asking God to show you how to pray in a way that pleases Him. Then pray slowly and thoughtfully asking the Holy Spirit to direct your prayer.

Day 5
Read Psalm 35.

1. What does David mean when he says, "Contend, O LORD, with those who contend with me"?
2. What phrases in this psalm reveal what he wants God to do with these people?
3. Do you consider this an imprecatory psalm? Why, or why not?

4. What would you want to know about yourself before you made such a request as verse 1 to God?
5. Who might you be tempted to pray the words of verse 1 about?
6. Read Matthew 5:43–45. Spend some of today's prayer time praying *for* that person, not *against* him or her.

Day 6
Read Psalm 9.

1. Find as many references as you can to "the nations."
2. What emphasis does David make with this frequent repetition?
3. How is David's view of international events different from people who do not know God? (See especially verses 7 and 8.)
4. How does David perceive his country's position among the nations of the world?
5. According to this psalm, what do you think David sees as important ways to keep his nation under God's protection?
6. How do you think David might respond to God in a time of national crisis?
7. Pray today for your nation.

14

WHAT HAPPENS WHEN LEADERS STUMBLE?

1 Chronicles 21

How many national leaders can you name? Now drop to the state level? Local level? Do you have a grand total? (Was it less than you could number on both hands?)

Now think of the specific responsibilities each of these people carries. Which of these do you consider most critical? How do the decisions of these leaders affect you personally? What bearing do the decisions have on what you believe to be "right"? What moral issues emerge from their areas of responsibility?

If you think through these questions, you'll have a good start on today's discussion.

Read aloud 1 Chronicles 21:1–11.

1. What reasons might David have had for taking a census?

Helps for leaders can be found at the back of the book.

_____

_____

_____

2. What evidence in this chapter suggests that the people nearest these events believed that this particular census was wrong? _____

_____

_____

_____

3. What choices did God give David? _____

_____

_____

_____

4. If you had been David, what would you have chosen?

_____

Why? _____

_____

Read aloud 1 Chronicles 21:12–20.

5. What did David choose? _____

_____

Why? _____

_____

6. What would you need to believe about God in order to cast yourself on Him in this way? _____

_____

_____

_____

_____

7. What words and actions indicate the severity of the plague? _____

_____

_____

   What events show that the writer of 1 Chronicles believed the plague to be a direct act of God?

_____

_____

8. What steps did David take to offer a proper sacrifice to God? _____

_____

_____

9. How did David know that God honored his prayer?

_____

10. What decision points do you find for David in this chapter? _____

_____

_____

_____

    Which of these would you call wise and which unwise decisions? _____

_____

_____

11. What points can you recall in your own nation's history where a national leader's decision had far-reaching effects on the people of your country? _____

_____

_____

_____

12. What do you think we ought to ask God for when we pray for our national leaders? _____

_____

_____

_____

13. Spend a few moments praying sentence prayers for your nation and its leaders. Pray for these leaders by name.

THROUGH THE WEEK

Day 1
Read Psalm 122.

1. How does David feel about his nation's capital, Jerusalem?
2. What blessings does he ask God for Jerusalem?
3. What reasons are suggested here for David's returning the ark of God to Jerusalem, when he had to flee the city (2 Samuel 15:25–26)?
4. Why might God have stopped the plague after David's census, just before it reached Jerusalem (1 Chronicles 21:15)?
5. What needs exist in your own nation's capital?
6. Spend time today praying for your own capital city.

Day 2
Read Psalm 108.

1. How does David intend to praise God? (verses 1–5)
2. If David believes God's words of verses 7–9, how might they keep him from pride in a high census figure?
3. In what ways does David express the idea that his military strength is not in large armies, but in God?
4. Spend some time searching out before God your own values. Do you place too much value on particular items or things that belong to you? Do you depend too much on people or even one person for your own stability and well-being? If you are able, release these to God in prayer and put Him first.

Day 3
Read Psalm 38.

1. What words describe David's physical condition?

2. What fears does he express?
3. What does David consider the cause of his misery?
4. Notice each time that he addresses God directly. How does David express a dependence on God?
5. If David prayed this prayer for his people during a time of plague, what would you expect God to do?
6. What comfort can you find in the words of verse 9? Spend some time today expressing your own "longings" and "sighings" to God. Close your prayer with the words of verses 21 and 22.

Day 4
Read Psalm 25.

1. Find as many notes of praise to God as you can in this psalm.
2. In what ways does David express submission to God?
3. Why might mentally reviewing God's character, then purposely subjecting ourselves to God's rule, be a healthy activity in times of crisis?
4. How does David's prayer deal with the possibility that his troubles are at least partially a result of his own sin?
5. Can we expect God's help even when we have brought trouble on ourselves? Why, according to this psalm?
6. How does David express the idea that his praise and his petitions are not merely on his own behalf?
7. What might you draw from this psalm in a time of crisis?

Day 5
Read Psalm 31.

1. Find as many verses as you can that seem to reflect some event in David's past.
2. What experiences do you think led David to say, "My times are in your hands"?

3. What must David believe about God in order to say this?
4. What changes would have to come in your thinking or actions for you to make that kind of statement?
5. If these words of commitment are already true for you, what effect should they have on the way you use your time today?

Day 6
Read 2 Samuel 22–23:7.

1. Divide the poem of chapter 22 into about 10 stanzas. Note an event in David's life for which each paragraph seems appropriate.
2. Find a stanza that seems to speak particularly to your current circumstances. Meditate on it. Then talk to God about how this passage affects you.
3. Glance through the thumbnail sketches of David's military leaders in 2 Samuel 23:8–23. What visual images do these word pictures create? What kinds of men surrounded David?
4. Read slowly David's final words in 2 Samuel 23:1–7. What clues do you find that David feels ready to die?
5. From David's description of himself in verse 1, what did he think was important in his life?
6. Examine verses 2–5. What does David see as important about his writing, his ruling, his family?
7. Look at *one* of these same areas in your own life (your words, your authority, your family). How might you model the values David expresses in these verses?
8. What encouragement might you find in these seven verses to set your life on a God-centered path?
9. What steps could you be taking now that would help you feel satisfaction when your life is finished?

15

HOW DO GOD'S SERVANTS DIE?

1 Chronicles 22, 28–29*

Do God's people die any differently than the rest of the world's population? Does a servant of God look back at his past with anything more than a sighed, "When it's over, it's over"? At his death, does he look at the future (his own and those he leaves behind) with any more confidence than his pagan neighbors?

As for David, would you expect him to be so weighted down by his own sin that he would approach death with fear? Or would you expect his long walk with God to carry him triumphantly through death?

And what about you? How might David's living help you cope with dying?

Read aloud 1 Chronicles 22.

1. What preparations did David make for his death? (Look now for major categories, not small details.)

Helps for leaders can be found at the back of the book.

*The First Chronicles account of David's death and Solomon's ascendance to the throne emphasizes the religious nature of this occasion. For the political maneuverings surrounding these events, read 1 Kings 1 and 2.

_____

_____

_____

2. What link does the first verse provide between this chapter and the previous one? _____

_____

3. What hint does David's inability to build the temple give about God's view of the violence surrounding David's life? _____

_____

*4. What had God promised Solomon? _____

_____

_____

_____

_____

*5. What practical preparations did David make for building the temple? _____

_____

_____

_____

_____

6. What spiritual counsel did David give his son and his people? _____

_____

_____

_____

*optional question

_____

_____

_____

7. If you were to pass on one note of spiritual counsel to your children, what would you tell them?

_____

_____

Read aloud 1 Chronicles 28.

8. What purposes do you think David had for calling this public assembly? _____

_____

_____

9. What principles of personal spiritual development emerge from David's counsel? _____

_____

_____

_____

*10. How did David encourage Solomon and the people to get on with the job of building the temple?

_____

_____

_____

Read aloud 1 Chronicles 29.

11. How does David's prayer elaborate on the theme of verse 14, "Everything comes from you"?

_____

_____

_____

_____

12. Why might this attitude about ownership bring about a satisfying life? _____

_____

_____

*13. Think back over David's life. What reasons did he have to face death with contentment? _____

_____

_____

_____

_____

*14. What are some of your concerns about your own life coming to an end? _____

_____

_____

_____

15. How might David's belief that God is "ruler of all things" (verse 12) help you approach death—whenever it comes? _____

_____

_____

_____

_____

THROUGH THE WEEK

Day 1
Read Psalm 37.

1. Look carefully at verses 1–9. Find 6 actions (or instructions not to act) in these verses.
2. David says in verse 25, "I was young and now I am old." As you think back over David's wide experiences, what incentive do you have to take these six proverbs of advice seriously.
3. This week, select one of these proverbs for each day. Try to live out that proverb throughout the day. Make some notes about your experiences.
4. Look at verses 10–38. Make a two-column chart. List David's observations about the wicked on one side, his observations about the righteous on the other.
5. As you look at these lists, what reasons can you find to obey God's commands?
6. Read verses 39–40. According to these verses, how is salvation different from being good enough to please God?
7. Thank God today that salvation comes, not from yourself, but "from the LORD."

Day 2
Read Psalm 39.

1. Why did David endure a period of silence?
2. When he spoke, what did he ask God?
3. What words does David use to describe his life?
4. Why did life, at that point, seem futile to him?
5. In spite of this feeling of futility, what qualities in God do you think he remembers in order to say in verse 7, "My hope is in you"?

6. What events near the end of David's life would you consider an answer to his prayer of verse 13?
7. What reasons do you have to be glad that God, not man, is in charge of the length of your life?
8. Think a few moments about the unknown span of days ahead of you. Say to God with David, if you can, "My hope is in you."

Day 3
Read Psalm 13.

1. If you were to place this psalm at some point in David's past, where would you place it? Why?
2. Why, in David's opinion, has his life lasted this long?
3. What reasons does he have for hope even during hardship?
4. Read again verse 6. Think of some ways in which God has been good to you. Thank Him for these.

Day 4
Read Psalm 20.

1. Why might David have used this prayer when Soloman became king?
2. What does David see as a basis for any success as king?
3. When you have a difficult job ahead of you, what kinds of "chariots and horses" (verse 7) are you tempted to trust instead of God?
4. How might you follow the teaching of verse 5 in that situation and "lift up your banners in the name of God?"
5. Think of one difficult task that faces you today. Honestly try to do that job in God's name and through His strength.

Day 5
Read Psalm 110.

1. Which of the phrases in this psalm might apply to David?
2. Which might also refer to Jesus Christ?
3. What evidence can you find in verse 1 that Jesus Christ existed before He was born in Bethlehem? (See also Mark 12:36–37 and Acts 2:29–35.)
4. In what sense has Jesus Christ become your "priest forever" (Psalm 110:4)?
5. Talk to Jesus, your priest, today. Thank Him for His eternal sacrifice.

Day 6
Read Psalm 8.

1. Read this psalm several times until the words almost follow each other automatically.
2. According to this psalm, which of God's created works echo His glory?
3. What comparisons does David draw between man and the rest of God's creation?
4. What does David find surprising about the position God has given man?
5. How might this psalm affect the way you view the rest of God's creation? (Consider your use or misuse of nature; your knowledge of birds, trees, rocks, flowers, the sea, stars; the time you spend enjoying God's creation.)
6. Memorize some portion of this psalm.

16

WHAT WAS DAVID'S PHILOSOPHY OF LIFE?

Psalm 139

Have you been with us from the beginning?

If so, you have studied all of David's life and all of his known writings: 43 narrative chapters and 73 psalms. You've contributed to 16 discussions and prayed through 90 personal quiet times with God.

You've seen the boy David secretly anointed king. You've run with David from King Saul and later from his own son, Absalom. You've watched David conquer a huge territory and rule as king over it. You've observed his secret sin and his public punishment. You've felt his remorse and his forgiveness. Then you've watched him die.

The New Testament calls David "a man after God's own heart." So as a climax to our study, we might profitably ask, "What did such a man believe?" To answer this, we look at Psalm 139. There David writes what he believes to be true about God, about man, and about life. It is perhaps his greatest written work.

Helps for leaders can be found at the back of the book.

Read Psalm 139:1–6.

1. What everyday examples does David use to illustrate God's knowledge? _____

   _____

   _____

   _____

2. How does David express the idea that God knows more than he himself does? _____

   _____

   _____

3. Why might some people feel uncomfortable that anyone, even God, knows them that well? _____

   _____

   _____

   How does this differ from David's attitude about God's knowledge? _____

   _____

Read verses 7–12.

4. What new quality of God's does David introduce in this stanza? _____

   _____

5. When might a person, even a godly person, want to run from God? _____

   _____

   _____

   _____

6. Why might such a person be glad in the long run that God is inescapable? _____

_____

_____

Read verses 13–16.

7. According to these verses, when does God begin to care about a person? _____

_____

What basis do these verses give for a sense of personal worth? _____

_____

_____

8. Jot down three physical or personality traits that you like about yourself and three that you do not like.

_____

_____

_____

_____

_____

Without necessarily sharing what you wrote, how might these verses help you deal with the traits you don't like?

_____

_____

_____

_____

How might these verses also prevent you from unwarranted pride? _____

_____

9. What effect might these verses have on the way you approach sickness and death? _____

_____

_____

Read verses 17–18.

10. According to these verses, what can we know and not know about God? _____

_____

_____

Read verses 19–22.

11. In what respect is David taking sides at this point in his prayer? _____

_____

_____

Read verses 23–24.

12. What does David ask God to do here?

_____

_____

_____

13. As you think through the entire psalm, in what three major directions has David aimed his attention?

_____

Why is each a natural outgrowth of the other?

_____

_____

Reread the entire psalm aloud.

14. What does this psalm reveal of David's philosophy of life? _____

_____

_____

_____

15. How might the previous stanzas of the prayer make it easier for us to honestly pray the ending?

_____

_____

_____

16. What might we expect to happen if we pray the prayer of verses 23–24? _____

_____

_____

_____

HELPS FOR LEADERS

1 / IS ANYONE IN CHARGE UP THERE?

1 Samuel 16

Q1, 2. Encourage each person to contribute a different answer. If your group is accustomed to using a study guide where each question has only one correct answer, they'll have some difficulty making the shift to discussion questions. You can shorten this transition period by announcing that each question has several answers. Then after each response ask, "Does anyone see something else?" "Have we missed anything?" Or, "Does everyone agree with what Sue said?" and so on.

Note: In certain translations of the Bible, there are four books called Kings and none named Samuel. In these, 1 Samuel is titled 1 Kings.

Q3. Potential answers include:
- —God's concern about Samuel's grief (v. 1)
- —His provision for a new king of Israel (v. 1)
- —His plan for Samuel's welfare during the trip to Bethlehem (vv. 2–5)

—God's knowledge of the inner person (v. 7)

—His detailed communication with Samuel while Jesse's sons passed by (vv. 6–12)

—The descent of God's Spirit on David from that day forward (v. 13)

Q6. See verse 7.

Q7, 8. Be sensitive to the needs of your people as they respond to these questions. Take time to wait, thereby encouraging several to speak. Since we are much more likely to carry through good intentions that we spell out in words, help group members be as specific as possible. Take care, however, not to invade anyone's privacy.

Q9. Answers appear throughout verses 14–23. Help your group to stick to the job of finding them.

Q11. Encourage the group to mention the changes as they appear in the passage.

Note: Several people are likely to express concern about the phrase "evil spirit from God" (verses 14, 16, 23). A discussion of this phrase can stimulate serious thought about the nature of God, so allow time to talk it over. Be careful, however, that this controversy does not fill your remaining time. If the group is unable to settle on a satisfactory meaning of the phrase, you can table the discussion with these possible explanations, then firmly direct attention to the next question.

1) The evil spirit was a spirit of gloomy suspicious melancholy, bordering on madness, affecting the mind of Saul. To the Hebrews, every visitation, good or evil, came directly from God. (Pfeiffer and Harrison, *Wycliffe Bible Commentary*, p. 286)

2) The evil spirit was *not* a supernatural evil being, but a judgment of God on Saul because of his sin. (Jack B. Scott, *An Old Testament Survey, God's Plan Unfolded*, p. 126)

3) An evil spirit filled the place vacated by God's Spirit. Because God's Spirit departed, an evil power took possession

of Saul and at times drove him to madness. Since the depar-
ture of God's Spirit initiated this condition, the evil spirit
could be referred to as "from God." In fact, God sent it as a
punishment. (Keil and Delitzsch, *Commentary on the Old
Testament*, p. 179)

Q13. This is a summary and review question. A quick
reference to several phrases from the chapter should help
center your thoughts on God's provision for His people. Answers given to questions 3 and 9 may help form a basis.

Q14. Save about ten minutes for this question so that each
person who is willing can respond to it fully. End your study
time by drawing your group together in praying for each other
about some of the circumstances they have mentioned. Acknowledge to God his authority over all of them.

Note: At the close of the study, point out the six studies
under the heading "Through the Week" and the note regarding them at the end of today's discussion questions. These
quiet time studies form the heart of your study of David.
Encourage people to participate in them by keeping a personal notebook to record their findings, thoughts, and
prayers.

2 / ARE MY BATTLES GOD'S BATTLES?

1 Samuel 17

Q1. Select a fluent reader who has a modern translation
and ask her to read the story from beginning to end. Then
linger on the first question as your group recalls and enjoys
together the colorful details of the story. Don't try to evaluate
the events now; that will occur later in the study.

Note: Sometime during this study, a group member is
likely to raise a question about the violence surrounding

David's life. No simple answer exists, particularly when that violence seems God-ordered or God-sanctioned. The best way to handle the subject is to acknowledge that violence is in fact a major part of the story. (The Bible never glosses ugly details.) You can also note that the enemy tribes surrounding Israel were even more violent. They practiced torture and child sacrifices. Suggest that God's view of this violence may become more clear as the study progresses. (See especially study 15 for 1 Chronicles 22.)

A long discussion of violence versus pacifism or the Old Testament God of wrath versus the New Testament God of love will likely prove unprofitable except to note that God Himself does not change. We must therefore integrate both views of God into what we believe to be true about Him.

Q2. See verses 12–14, 17–22, and 28–29. Do not expect your group to merely recite the facts here. These may have appeared in question 1. But look for feelings and status within the family structure.

Q3. See verses 32–40. Contrast the information and general tone here with what you discovered in question 2.

Q4. Note David's references to God in verses 26 and 37. Then help the group draw from them who David thought God to be. Discuss how this differed from the view of the soldiers, the Philistines, even from his own brothers, and from King Saul. Talk about why this knowledge of God allowed David to take unusual risks with confidence.

Q6. See verses 9, 16, and 25–26.

Q9, 10. Pace the study so that you allow your group enough time to thoughtfully discuss these questions. Ten or fifteen minutes is not too much time. Most group members will feel comfortable responding to question 9. When they have discussed that question as long as seems profitable, read question 10 and allow a few moments of silence before continuing the discussion.

Some people may have trouble defining a "battle" in their own lives. Looking back at the paragraph introducing this study may help. If is seems appropriate at the end, pray together for those who have revealed their current battles.

Note: Why did Saul ask, "Whose son is that young man?" (verse 55), when Saul had already experienced a long acquaintance with David (16:14–23)? Bible commentators offer several solutions:

1) David had grown older and changed in appearance so Saul did not recognize him. (Blaikie, p. 19)
2) Saul knew David but now that David would become his son-in-law, he wanted to know his family. (Blaikie, p. 19)
3) Saul was inquiring about the social status of David's family. (Keil and Delitzsch, p. 186)
4) This chapter is a flashback, recounting an event prior to the happenings in chapter 16.
5) First Samuel 16:21–23 is a summary statement covering chapters 16–20 and not a specific act told in sequence.
6) Saul's unstable mental state caused him not to recognize David.
7) Saul had not seen David as a person before, but merely as a tool to serve his needs.

3 / WHAT MAKES A GOOD FRIEND?

1 Samuel 20

Today's passage forms a rather long narrative. Begin promptly to allow ample time for reading. It will save time if you read the first question before having the passage read. This will allow group members to spot answers during the reading.

Q1. Expect at least one answer from each participant. Be sure they cite chapter and verse so that people with differing translations can keep together.

Q2. Ingredients of the friendship will grow out of the previous question, but answers here should move beyond, ''The passage says . . .'' and on to ''that event means . . .''.

Ingredients people may notice in the friendship include: mutual trust, dependence, loyalty, encouragement. These ingredients enabled the two men to take risks for each other, make hard promises, show their emtions, and put their friendship under God's rule.

Q3. Several barriers appear in this passage:

—Saul, Jonathan's father, was a political opponent to David.

—Jonathan was crown prince, yet David had been anointed king by the prophet Samuel.

—Jonathan wanted to respect and believe his father.

—Since Jonathan and David were close friends, they wanted to be together, yet this might endanger David's life.

David and Jonathan overcame these barriers in several ways:

—David did not force his opinion on Jonathan in order to discover Saul's true position. Instead, they set up a situation where Jonathan could see for himself.

—David asked Jonathan's permission to leave (20:5).

—Jonathan acknowledged David as future king (20: 13–15).

—David gave appropriate honor to Jonathan as crown prince (20:41).

—Jonathan's actions of 18:3–4 must have borne political and personal significance. (Note: according to 1 Samuel 13:22, there were only two swords in the kingdom.)

Your group may want to mention these items, then go on to

discuss general principles by which these men worked out friendship in a difficult setting.

Q4. See chapter 20, verses 18–22 and 35–40. The men probably thought that if Saul were as hostile as David suspected, they might be prevented from further personal communication. As it worked out, Jonathan was able to send the boy away so that he and David could have a final conversation.

Q5. See Jonathan's promises in verses 4, 9, 12–15, 42 and David's in 14–15 and 42. Take careful note of these as they come up again in 2 Samuel 9.

Q8. See verses 13–14 and 42. Perhaps your group will also find other evidences in the passage.

Note: Was the friendship of David and Jonathan a homosexual relationship?

Some critics have said yes, particularly in view of 2 Samuel 1:26 where David in mourning Jonathan's death declares,

> "Your love for me was wonderful, more wonderful than that of women."

Yet there is evidence to the contrary. In the same psalm of mourning, David says, in verse 23

> "Saul and Jonathan—
>> in life they were loved and gracious, and in death they were not parted."

These words may be hyperbole (a deliberate exaggeration for effect). If so, his words about Jonathan's love may be similar.

In addition, both men planned children (1 Samuel 20:42) and in fact fathered several each.

Finally, it is hard to imagine two men taking an oath under God's authority while at the same time violating God's law against homosexual behavior (Leviticus 20:13).

Don't bring up the issue of homosexuality unless your group does. But if the subject pops into the discussion, simply present the evidence in brief form, then direct the attention back to the main track.

Q9, 10, 11. Leave about fifteen minutes to discuss these final questions of application.

If people are slow to respond to question 10, review some of their answers to question 1 as jumping off points for discussing the pluses and minuses of deep friendship.

4 / REVENGE OR RECONCILIATION?

1 Samuel 23–24

Q1. Don't spend a lot of time here; brief summary comments that set the stage for study are what you need.

Q2. Each group member should participate. Ask that they quickly cite one event and the verse, then go on to another person.

Q3. See verses 2, 11, 12, 14, and 26–27.

Note: An ephod (v. 9) was a simple linen garment worn by the priests. A special ephod, however, hung in the temple and was used only by the high priest. It contained the urim and thummin, probably two flat objects used in casting lots. Evidently, this was the ephod Abiathar brought with him when he fled to David. (*New Bible Dictionary*, p. 326 and 1306)

"It is evident from verses 9–12, that when the will of God was sought through the urim and thummin, the person making the inquiry placed the matter before God in prayer, and received an answer; but always to one particular question." (Keil and Delitzsch, p. 229–230.) King Saul used this device in 1 Samuel 14:36–43.

Q4. See especially 1 Samuel 23 verses 14–18.

Q5. Let your group explore several routes of action. Among them, David could have killed Saul; he could have confronted him on the spot; he could have ignored him, never letting Saul know he and his men had been in the back of the same cave.

Let your group speak briefly of the probable outcome of each of these action.

Q6. Draw several points from verses 8–15.

Q7. See verses 16–21.

Q8. Your group should note that David had already made this same promise to Jonathan in 1 Samuel 20:14–17, 42 and 1 Samuel 23:16–18. They may think of other reasons too.

Q9. Note David's caution in verse 22.

Q12. If your group spent a great deal of time with question 8, they may have answered this one already. If so, just skip it and go on to question 13.

Be sure, however, that they have touched on the positive steps toward reconciliation. David did not merely refuse revenge. He went to a lot of trouble to make the relationship right.

Q13. See verses 6, 12, and 15. But go beyond the facts of the verses. Look at what David believed to be God's nature and why he might have taken these actions because of that nature.

Q14, 15. Allow about ten minutes for thoughtful exploration of these questions.

Caution: Don't assume that all broken relationships ought to be mended. For instance, God would not expect that a victim of beatings from her husband initiate reconciliation if she were almost certain that her husband would beat her again.

5 / WHO WAS DAVID'S GOD?

Psalm 62

Psalm 62 is often associated with a later period in David's life (2 Samuel 12:7–13). Yet, the spiritual battle for David when he fled from Saul was much the same as when he fled from Absalom. One quarter through the study of David's life seems an appropriate time to examine together one of David's prayers of worship. Here we can see through David's eyes, "Who was David's God?"

The tone of this study should be thoughtful and meditative. Your group may have gotten used to galloping through a long narrative passage. If so, you'll need to slow them down for this study. (Don't let thoughtful silence make you feel uncomfortable.) Take time to linger over these twelve verses so that you can better worship the God of David.

Q2. Don't stop to discuss these characteristics now. They will come up later in the study. For now, settle for a brief description and the verse where the characteristic is found. Try to involve each person present in some part of the answer.

—God is a rock (vv. 2, 6, 7).
—He is a fortress (vv. 2, 6).
—He is (or gives) salvation (vv. 1, 2, 6, 7).
—God is a refuge (vv. 7, 8).
—God is strong (v. 11).
—He is loving (v. 12).
—God speaks (v. 11).
—He rewards (v. 12).
—God gives rest (vv. 1, 5).
—He gives hope (v. 5).
—God can be trusted (v. 8).

Be sure that your group takes note of all these characteristics since you will use them throughout the study.

Q3. Parallelism is a characteristic of Hebrew poetry. The same idea is repeated in different ways with different shades of meaning. Verses 1 and 2 are in parallel with verses 5 and 6. Within the verses other parallels occur. Line 2 of verse 2 parallels line 1 of the same verse, and so forth. In some sense the words *rock, fortress, refuge, salvation* all parallel each other and David uses their similar meanings to build his poetic structure. But the careful reader should not dismiss the similar words as mere repetition varied only for the sake of form. Each word reveals a different shade of the character of God.

Encourage the group to form mental images of these words and discuss how these qualities relate to God's character.

Q4. Help the group refer back to David's experiences thus far in the account of his life. For example, since he was hunted many times by King Saul, he must have often needed rest and refuge in a literal sense. Perhaps God also provided these to his inner spirit.

Q6. See verses 3, 4, and 9.

Q8. See verses 9 and 10.

Q10. Try to keep discussion of this question rooted in the passage. (For example, God is all-knowing, but that quality isn't mentioned here.) Contrast the qualities of God noted in response to question 2 with the qualities of people, of prestige, of power, and of money.

Q11, 12, 13. Stress personal responses to God here. The most valuable answers will begin with the word "I," not "we" or "they." Don't be alarmed by a brief silence. These questions should provoke thoughtful meditation. Allow time to think, then ask the group members to share some of their thoughts. Areas of response should emphasize meaningful ways to worship God in times of personal need.

6 / CAN I CREATE PEACE?

1 Samuel 25

Q1. Your group may discover these or similar characteristics from the following verses:

David	Abigail	Nabal
hot tempered (v. 13)	intelligent (v. 3)	surly and mean (v. 3)
forethoughtful (vv. 7–8)	beautiful (v. 3)	foolish (v. 25)
vengeful (vv. 21–33)	decisive (v. 18)	drunken (v. 36)
reasonable (vv. 32–34)	diplomatic (vv. 26–31)	cowardly or vulnerable (v. 37)
opportunistic (v. 40)	inciteful (vv. 26–31)	
	practical (v. 36)	
	opportunistic (v. 41)	

Q2. The answer to this question is not clearly stated but the implications are that David wanted provisions or a share in the profit of sheep shearing.

Q3. Help your group examine both responses to David's request. Nabal referred to David as a possible runaway slave. He obviously hadn't heard of David even though David had been camped around Nabal's property with six hundred men.

Yet the servants, who had been on the scene, thought David's request was reasonable. They did not view it as extortion.

Q4. Explore several choices open to Abigail and their probable results.

Q5. Short honest answers are what you want here.

Q6. See the details of verse 18.

Q7, 8. Find about eight answers to question 7 in verses 23–31. Don't elaborate on these as you work on question 7, but as you move into question 8, use these facts to interpret Abigail's insights.

Q9. See verses 19, 36, 37.

Q10. Use the several references to God in this chapter as a basis for answers. Note particularly the poetic language of verse 29 and its possible allusion to the Goliath event.

Q11. Group memebers should spot several examples of God's provision for David and Abigail. They might note:

—Abigail married a good husband.

—Her servants were spared.

—David acquired property in Judah.

—He got a sensible and diplomatic wife.

—David's soldiers were given food.

—Abigail was released from a foolish husband.

Q12. Use answers to the previous two questions to probe further into the nature of God as it relates to the way group members respond to hostile situations. They might want to think back to their answers for question 5.

Q13. This question too reflects back to question 5, but it also looks at Abigail's adept handling of a volatile situation and looks ahead at general principles we may use in our own hostile environments. Discussion should uncover some of the following ideas:

Genuine peace cannot come from simply covering up the hostility. In the same way, you don't solve the problem by distracting a two-year-old away from a valuable trinket. Eventually the child must learn that he cannot handle and break this.

Genuine peace cannot come from ignoring the conflict, as Nabal tried.

It cannot come from personal revenge, as was David's plan.

Genuine peace does not come when one person allows himself to be squashed by another so that he avoids open conflict but endures long-term simmering hostility (and possible ulcers).

Genuine peace does not come when we run in fear from hostility.

Genuine peace will come when we handle a situation much as Abigail did. We evaluate it realistically. (Don't pretend it is either more or less serious than it really is.) Then we deal openly with the problem, placing it under God's control and using methods as compatible as we are able with God's nature and purpose.

Q14. Pause after reading the first sentence of this question until you are sure that everyone has a specific situation in mind. Then encourage people to share one specific step toward peace. Be sure to allow opportunity to discuss this question, but set a tone that does not invade privacy or invite gossip.

At the close of the study, point out that this week's Through the Week assignments are narratives that move forward in the story of David's life. Anyone who does not read these may feel a little lost in next week's group discussion.

7 / DO I TRY TO PLAY GOD?

1 Samuel 31–2 Samuel 2:7

Q1. See verses 2–6. Since these details vary with the account in 2 Samuel, be sure that your group spots them and recounts them accurately.

—The Philistines killed Saul's sons (v. 2).

—The archers wounded Saul critically (v. 3).

—Saul tried to get his own armor-bearer to kill him (v. 4).

—The armor-bearer refused (v. 4)

—The armor-bearer saw that Saul was dead (v. 5).

Q2. In addition to the deaths of Saul and his sons, find several other actions throughout the chapter. Encourage group members to cite verses with each action they point out.

Q3. See 1 Samuel 27:7–12; 28:1; 29:1–4; 30:1–8, 18–20.

Q4. David suffered the loss of his good friend Jonathan, but he also suffered great political loss. The kingdom he was about to inherit was weakened. Much land had fallen to the Philistines. The nation of Israel had been humiliated. Furthermore, the Philistines, their long-standing enemy, had the advantage of momentum—they were on a winning streak.

Q6. Contrast the details of verses 6–10 with your observations in question 1.

The Amalekite must have stayed close enough to the action to see what was going on, then doctored the story to put himself in what he thought would be good standing with David. If David was to be the new king (and he had brought David the symbols of kingship) this Amalekite wanted a top spot. (A parallel account, however, in 1 Chronicles 10:1–6 accepts the 1 Samuel 31 version.)

Q7. See verses 15–16. Notice that the Amalekite died by execution, not by murder. In his role as king, David ordered the execution. But he did not do so on impulse. Verse 12 records that most of a day had past.

Q8. Some readers find David's lament over Saul's death hypocritical in view of the fact that David had spent the greater part of his life running from Saul. Others see hyperbole (purposeful exaggeration) here. Don't discourage people in your group who hold these ideas.

It seems likely, however, that David's lament represents a larger view than his own personal well-being. For example,

Saul and Jonathan were not parted in death. In spite of personal friendship with David, Jonathan had chosen to stay with his father. In addition, Saul and Jonathan were no doubt loved by some and gracious to some. Help the group examine the lament for this larger perspective.

Q9. This spare account of "just the facts" is quite a contrast to the visual language of 1 Samuel 16. Let your group speculate about the reasons. Answers might include:

—The nation was in mourning because of their fallen king. (No one made much comment about Lyndon B. Johnson's swearing in, either.)

—The nation was in trouble because of the battle losses. Anointing a new king was a minor detail.

—The true anointing (in God's sight) had already taken place. This public anointing was a mere formality.

—The writer might not have been present, so he merely recorded the facts as he heard them later.

Q10. Let your group browse through the account of David's life thus far. Temptation points might have occurred when David was in Saul's court (16:14–23), when he saw Saul in the cave (chapter 24), when Saul slept unprotected (chapter 26), when David acquired the property and manpower that had belonged to Nabal (chapter 25), when he was invited to accompany the Philistines to battle (29:1–2).

After the group has pointed out several of these incidents, let them talk about why David might now be relieved that he had waited.

Q11, 12. Save about fifteen minutes to discuss these final questions. Try to help group members speak personally, beginning their responses with the word "I."

8 / SHOULD I FEAR GOD?

2 Samuel 6

Q1. Expect your group to pick out six or eight answers to these verses.

Q3. David reacted in several ways and your group should note each. Verse 8 says David was angry. Verse 9 says he was afraid. He also seemed puzzled about the reason for Uzzah's death. He was concerned for the future, saying, "How can the ark of the Lord ever come to me." In the face of these emotional responses David responded with one action. He left the ark of God at the house of Obed-Edom. (Obed-Edom's name means "worshiper of Edom," *New Bible Commentary*, p. 304.) We can surmise, therefore, that this was a pagan home.

Q4. Encourage several people to interact with each other's ideas before proceeding to the references in the next question.

Q5, 6. Numbers 4:15 is God's command to Moses regarding the way the ark was to be transported. The 1 Chronicles passage is a parallel account of the way Uzzah died. Encourage group members to rethink their responses to question 4 in view of this added information. Then discuss the nature of God as displayed in these actions, and their own feelings about this part of God's nature.

Q8. In some ways David's preparation was similar. Note these. But the group should note also the following differences: David wore an ephod (a short priestly garment), he danced, he offered sacrifices, the ark was carried by men— not placed on a cart, David had prepared a tent for the ark, David blessed the people, then he sent them home with provisions of food.

Q10. This question calls for opinion answers and your group may express several. Some will feel that David exhibited righteous indignation—that his words to Michal were accurate, even prophetic, reflecting a true view of God's work in the past and his purpose for the future.

Others will see this as a temper fit, with the main purpose to hurt Michal.

The reasons for Michal having no children are equally open to dispute. Some may think that God cursed her because she misinterpreted David's dance to worship. Others will say that David simply refused further sex relations with her, so, of course, she was barren.

The purpose of these questions is not to have everyone agree on the motives, but, by discussing them, to examine the details of the passage. When that has been accomplished, move on to the next questions. Try to leave about fifteen minutes for the last three questions.

Note: An apparent contradiction to verse 23 occurs in 2 Samuel 21:8. Some translations refer there to Michal having five sons. Other translations insert the name Merab, Michal's sister (see 1 Samuel 14:49). Merab is probably correct. But scholars who use Michal's name compare 2 Samuel 6:23; 1 Samuel 18:19; and 2 Samuel 21:8. They say that the five sons were children of Merab and Adriel, but that Michal brought them up. Hence the confusion.

Q11. List several ways in which David and his people worshiped God. If the group fails to notice it, point out that part of their worship was obeying God by carrying the ark in the way He had commanded.

Q12. If your group is slow to respond to the second part of this question, try a more simple aspect of the question. For example, "Should we be afraid not to obey God?" Or, "Should we fear the consequences of disobeying God?"

A few may feel adamantly that our God does not invite fear, that the New Testament reveals Him as a God of love. The New Testament, however, also speaks of fearing God. See:

Luke 12:4–5, 2 Corinthians 5:10–11, 2 Peter 3:9–13, Revelation 14:9–10.

Don't take time from 2 Samuel to discuss these, but, if the issue seems important to people present, list the references and discuss them after today's lesson is finished, or prior to beginning your next study.

Opinions are certain to vary on this question, but if ideas differ significantly from the passage, ask people to try to reconcile their ideas with the events here.

Q13, 14. Fear of God is often described as a sense of awe that inspires worship. Yet, David's experience with the ark illustrates that fear of God is more than that. God is a God who gives commands—sets down rules for conduct. Because He is God, He can and does demand obedience. Twentieth century Christianity is not comfortable with the idea that our loving God is also a God of wrath. But He is. David saw it, and Uzzah experienced it.

The account in 2 Samuel 6 should cause each of us to look sharply at our own responses to God's commands. He really does expect us to obey. If we do not, we have every reason to fear Him.

9 / WHO PLANS MY LIFE?

2 Samuel 7

Ask a fluent expressive reader to read today's passages in the two sections indicated.

Q1. Help your group find several details in verses 1–3. If you like, also include information gained from chapter 6.

Q2. Find 3 answers to each of these questions.

Q4. Find 3 answers to part one in verses 10–11 and 7 answers to part two in verses 12–16.

Q8. Encourage several people to share experiences that have led them to this conclusion. But keep an eye on the clock. You should leave nearly half of your time to discuss the remainder of the study.

Q9. David speaks of himself as a *servant* throughout his prayer. Yet, this term is added to and further defined by his actions. He asks in verse 18, "Who am I," and "What is my family?" In verse 25, he submits to God's plan even though it is in conflict with his own. Verse 27 presents the rather startling statement that it took *courage* for David to pray.

Q10. David expresses a mixture of emotions. Expect the group to name these and point out phrases that show that emotion. For example, we see a comfortableness with God in verse 18. "David went in and sat before the Lord." Verse 19 expresses humility. In the following verses we see awe, thanksgiving, and praise.

Q11. For part one, pick out the details of verses 23–24.

Part two might inspire several different answers. Among them, this ordinary Hebrew might have thought that he (or his king) was in control—that he and his nation chose God, not the other way around.

Even if he accepted the idea that God was in control, he might see the purposes differently. He might see that for some reason God had chosen to make Israel great, but he might not see that God did this "for Himself, and to make a name for Himself" (v. 23).

Q12. Linger on this question until each major point of the prayer is worked into a definition of sovereignty.

Note: The term "O Sovereign Lord" appears in the New International Version of the Bible, among others. Some translations, however, use instead the phrase "LORD God." But in this context the word LORD implies sovereignty—as in the lord of a kingdom.

Q13. Leave about ten minutes to discuss this question.

10 / DOES MY SIN MATTER TO GOD?

2 Samuel 11–12

Q1. Lust, fear, distrust, determination, and grief are among the emotions that appear in this chapter.

Q4. Note 11:1 "the time when kings go off to war," Uriah's gentle chide in 11:11, and Joab's open threat in 12:26–28. It seems that King David had begun to enjoy the soft life a bit too much—and observers knew it.

Q5. See 2 Samuel 11:16–21. Notice Joab's minor revision of David's plot against Uriah—a revision that cost other lives. Note also his attempt to down play this tactical blunder when he sent back his report to David. Don't miss his thinly veiled threat in 12:26–28.

Q8. Help your group pick out the symbols. The rich man represents David; the poor man, Uriah. Bathsheba is the little ewe lamb.

Q9. Find six reasons in verses 7–8, including the statement, "And if all this had been too little, I would have given you even more."

Q10. See four results in verses 10–14.

Q11. Spend several minutes examining these words. Observations should include: the statement is an admission of personal guilt, *I* have sinned. It says that the action was *sin*, not just a mistake. It defines the sin as *against God*, not just against another person. The statement ascribes the name *Lord* to God, thereby acknowledging God's total authority over the person.

Q12. Opinions will vary here. Some may feel that God was unfair. Others will say that God forgave David, but that he still deserved punishment, perhaps to prevent future sin. Still others will say that David's punishment is an outgrowth of the kind of person he had become, so he had to live with the natural results of his sin.

Q14. The following verses may help answer this question: 12:5–6; 12:13; 12:20; 12:22–23; 12:24. Try to help the group find David's godly responses to Nathan's rebuke and to sickness and death in his own family. Don't leave out David's words in verses 22–23. It is one of the few Old Testament references to life after death.

Q15. Save at least ten minutes for these questions of personal application.

11 / DOES CONFESSION HAVE HEALING POWER?

Psalm 32

Moving from discussion of the narrative of David's life to a brief psalm will require a change of pace. Your group will be tempted to rush through these eleven verses as if there were thirty more verses to cover yet. So before you begin, point out that the passage is short and poetic in form, that you will slow down and study more thoughtfully than you would a long narrative passage.

Q1. Discuss the details of verses 3–4 and perhaps the phrase "mighty waters" of verse 6.

Caution: While David speaks of physical results of sin, we cannot assume that *all* physical illness is a direct result of sin. To do so might place unnecessary guilt on an ill person and at the same time discourage her from seeking needed medical help.

Q4. See verses 5–6. Several ingredients appear here, so don't stop with only one or two.

Q5. New International Version uses the word "cover" in both verses. Some other translations use different words but with similar meanings. Rephrase the question, if necessary, to accomodate these.

Q8. Look first at the details of verses 8–9, then turn to Psalm 51:13–15. (The group studied Psalm 51 in last week's Through the Week activities.)

Q9. Notice the comfort in Psalm 32:1–2, 6–7, 10. Notice also the demands of verses 8–9. Help the group discuss why these might be unsettling to their normal routine. They might look at areas such as decision making and plans for the future.

Q10. Some may want to talk about their experience with this week's Through the Week studies. If so, encourage these personal glimpses. Others may find that experience too recent for evaluative comment. They may want to talk about an experience of cleansing more distant in time. Encourage either kind of response.

Q11. The "righteous" person of verse 11 has been *declared* righteous. His sins are "covered" by God (v. 1) as an aftermath of repentance. It is not his own goodness that brings the rejoicing. Therefore, he can "rejoice in the Lord."

Q12, 13. Leave about ten to fifteen minutes for these questions. (Some may have partially answered question 12 when they talked about question 10.) Here they should expand on that and look at actual changes in behavior or circumstances rather than just the feeling of being cleansed.

12 / WHERE IS GOD WHEN MY WORLD CAVES IN?

2 Samuel 15–16

Be prepared to give a brief verbal summary of 2 Samuel 13–14 if most of your group members did not read it during the week.

Q3. *People*—David urged them to leave Jerusalem immediately (v. 14). He offered to let Ittai and the six hundred Gittites return to Jerusalem (v. 20).

Property—David left ten concubines to care for the palace (v. 16).

City of Jerusalem—David sent the ark back to the city (v. 25).

Q4. In addition to sending the ark back to Jerusalem, he also sent back two priests and their sons (vv. 27–29). He seemed to think they might be useful in sending messages back to him.

In verse 31, we find that David prayed that God would frustrate the counsel of Ahithophel, his chief counselor now gone over to Absalom's side.

Verses 32–37 show David sending his friend Hushai back to Absalom's house in order to infiltrate the court and counteract Ahithophel's advice. In addition, Hushai is to send messages to David by means of the priests' sons.

Verse 37 shows an answer to David's prayer of verse 31. Just as Absalom enters Jerusalem, so also does Hushai.

Q5. Review the great rejoicing that accompanied David's bringing the ark to Jerusalem, also the blessing it had brought Obed-Edom, and also Uzzah's death when the ark was not carried properly (2 Samuel 6). Since the ark symbolized God's presence, David must have felt terribly alone going out into the wilderness without it. He also might have feared that the blessing that seemed to accompany the ark of God might be bestowed on the city of Jerusalem and thereby on Absalom.

Yet, he expresses a view that God is bigger than the ark can contain. Verse 26 shows a belief that God may yet bring him back to Jerusalem, but if not, that God is still in control, and His way is best. Even in the midst of obvious calamity, David reflects submission to His God.

Q6. Encourage several moments of honest comments here.

Q8. Ziba, servant and caretaker for Mephibosheth, reports that Mephibosheth has gone over to Absalom's side. (For a history of David's relationship with Mephibosheth, review 1 Samuel 20:12–17 and 2 Samuel 9.) Ziba's report turned out later to be false (2 Samuel 19:24–20) but David had no way of knowing that at this point.

Note: Some translations use the name Miraballa here rather than Mephibosheth. This appears to be a shortened form of the same name.

Shimei's public cursing added to David's shame.

Ahithophel, David's top counselor, giving advice to Absalom added mental pain.

Of course, the public desecration of David's concubines was a crowning insult.

Q10. See 2 Samuel 15:12, 31–34 and 16:15, 21, 23.

Q12. See 2 Samuel 15:25–26 and 16:11–12. Some may wonder why David says in verse 11, "Let him curse, for the LORD has told him to."

Matthew Henry comments:

> As it was Shimei's sin, it was not from God, but from the devil and his own wicked heart, nor did God's hand in it excuse or extenuate it, much less justify it,. . . . But, as it was David's affliction, it was from the Lord, one of the evils which he raised up against him. David looked above the instrument of his trouble to the supreme director. (p. 529)

To clarify this point in your own mind, look ahead at 2 Samuel 19:15–23 where Shimei confesses guilt (though perhaps insincerely) and David forgives him. David could not have forgiven a person he did not believe to be guilty.

Q13. David's words and actions show that he still *believes* that God is present with him and in control of his life. But he had many reasons to *feel* abandoned by God. Your group may remember that in the midst of David's victories are the words, "The LORD gave David victories everywhere he went" (2 Samuel 8:14). So David could easily assume the reverse, though not necessarily true idea: defeat meant that God had abandoned him. 1 Samuel 18:14 contains a similar idea.

David also carried the memory of his sin with Bathsheba. Even though he knew that God forgave him, he might now doubt God's forgiveness and suspect that God had decided to separate Himself from David. (If your group questions whether this may, in fact, be what is happening, have them look again at God's promise in 2 Samuel 7:14–16.)

And David might look at the personal nature of his opposition. Absalom (his son), Ahithophel (his top counselor), Mephibosheth (Jonathan's son), all form the opposition. These people had all loved him in the past. He might easily project their unfaithfulness onto God and wonder if God also had abandoned him.

Q14. Allow enough time for several group members to respond to these questions. What would "cave in" differs from person to person, but death, divorce, and war are high on most lists. Since we may well deal with one or more of these in our lifetime, we would do well to think in advance how our view of God might sustain us at that time.

Be sure that your group discusses the last half of this question, since to end with the first half poses the problem but not the solution.

13 / WHERE IS GOD WHEN I FALL APART?

2 Samuel 18–19:8

Q1. Use this question to involve each person in the group in the conversation.

Q2. See verses 1–5.

Q3. See verses 6–18. Some participants may notice similarities in Absalom's death and Saul's death, but they will also find obvious differences.

Q4. Treat each of the three men separately as you analyze their conversation in verses 19–23. Look also at the way they told the news to David in verses 28–32.

Q5. See verses 24–33. Some of the vivid pictures in this scene may have come up in response to question 1. Now turn that same imagery into David's mind and talk over the emotional state these pictures reveal.

Q7. Everyone in your group should have some opinion about this question. Spend enough time for everyone to voice her ideas. Questions likely to emerge include: Was Joab justified in killing Absalom or was he trying to usurp David's authority?

Was Joab cool-headedly running the military end of the government while David fell apart emotionally, or was he cold, calculating, and unnecessarily cruel?

Did Joab have David's and the nation's best interest at heart, thinking that his harsh words and actions were precisely what David needed, or was he looking out for "number one"?

Don't expect everyone to agree (the commentaries don't either), but use this question to gain a careful look at Joab's character and the events surrounding Absalom's death.

Q8, 9. Your group may suggest several answers here. Some of them will likely conclude that Absalom would have eventually killed David, or had him killed, that there was no way the two leaders could coexist once Absalom had claimed the throne.

Others will notice that though Absalom was a strong military leader, his moral qualities would not have made him a good king. The people of Israel would have drifted away from God.

Q10, 11. Linger on these questions and allow people time to reflect back on past group studies and personal quiet time activities. Aim that each person respond in some way.

14 / WHAT HAPPENS WHEN LEADERS STUMBLE?

1 Chronicles 21

Q1. Group members should suggest several possible motives.

Q2. See Joab's hesitation in verses 3–6, David's response to receiving the final count in verse 8, and Gad's warning from God in verses 9–12. In addition, the tone of the writer suggests no surprise that this deed deserved punishment.

As for why it was wrong for David to take a census, we can only guess. God had not in the past forbidden it. In fact, God had instructed Moses to take a census (Numbers 1:1–4). Opinions abound. Keil and Delitzsch list seven possible explanations (pp. 501–502). Matthew Henry lists six more (pp. 570–571).

A long discussion of God's possible motives will likely prove fruitless to your group. It should be sufficient to note that the people closest to the situation (David, Joab, Gad, the writer) did not appear to think God's actions unjust. If members of your group seem dissatisfied with that, appoint someone to research the problem during the coming week, but for now, don't spend a lot of time on it. Proceed with the study.

Q3. See verse 12.

Q5. Note that David did not select one of the three options. Instead he ruled out fleeing from his enemies for three months. He left the remainder of the choice to God.

Q6. Verse 13 refers to God's mercy. Note this, then encourage group members to speak of other attributes of God that would help them make that kind of choice.

Q7. Find several words and actions in verses 14–24 that show the severity of the plague. Don't forget to look at people's response to the angel of the Lord. Notice also that David had just counted 1,100,000 fighting men. Now 70,000 people are dead. It is not clear whether these 70,000 are fighting men only or if they are a total from the general population. If they represent fighters only, David had lost nearly one-twentieth of his people.

Q8. See the details of verses 18–24.

Q9. See verses 26–27. Turn also to 2 Samuel 24:25, if your group is interested.

Q10. Help your group find and discuss several throughout the chapter.

Q11. Leave about fifteen minutes for the final three questions. This will require you to pace carefully the early part of the study.

Use a tight rein for question 11. What you need here is about three brief examples, not a long political analysis. Conserve your time, leaving time for the final two questions.

Q12, 13. Encourage as many as are willing to participate in these final questions and prayer.

Note: This vivid account of David's census appears in two places: here in 1 Chronicles 21 and also in 2 Samuel 24. While the gist of the story remains the same in each telling, several differences will become apparent if your group compares the two passages. These points and possible explanations appear below:

1) Who incited David to take a census?

First Chronicles says Satan did. Second Samuel attributes this to God.

Both are likely true. "In the Old Testament, Satan, however evil, is an angel of God, a minister of God, a being who has only as much power as God entrusts to him" (*New Bible Commentary*, p. 379).

Similarly, "Satan, as an enemy, suggested it for a sin. . . . God, as righteous Judge, permitted it, with a design, from this sin of David, to take an occasion to punish Israel for other sins, for which he might justly have punished them" (Matthew Henry, p. 571).

2) How many people did the census number?

First Chronicles counts 1,100,000 while 2 Samuel records 1,300,000.

New Bible Commentary found no satisfactory attempt to reconcile the two numbers and suggests an early textual error (pp. 379, 314).

3) How much did David pay for Araunah's property?

First Chronicles says six hundred shekels but 2 Samuel calls for only fifty shekels.

The Chronicles price probably included the site surrounding the threshing floor (*New Bible Commentary*, p. 380).

4) How did David know that God had accepted his sacrifice?

First Chronicles speaks of fire from heaven, while 2 Samuel says simply, ''The plague on Israel was stopped.'' Both probably occurred.

15 / HOW DO GOD'S SERVANTS DIE?

1 Chronicles 22, 28–29

Today's study covers lengthy reading material, so pace the study carefully to allow extra time for reading. Since the passage speaks for itself, you may safely omit some of the optional questions.

Q1. Allow your group to mention several caregories but don't dwell on them at this point. You will discuss them more fully later in the study.

Q2. Notice that Araunah's threshing floor, purchased by David during the plague, became the future site of Solomon's temple.

Q3. Your group should remember from 2 Samuel 7 David's intention to build the temple. The writer did not there give a reason why God would not permit David to build, and Solomon had not yet been born. But God made strong promises to David's yet unnamed son. David's prayer at that time testified that he accepted God's limitations and believed the promises.

Q4. Find several points in 1 Chronicles 22:9 and 10.

Q5. Notice the details of 22:1–4, 14–18; and 23:1–5. Don't spend undue time on this.

Q6. See verses 11–13 for David's counsel to his son and verse 19 for his exhortation to his people.

Q7. Linger here as much as you are able and still allow time to finish the study.

Q8. The group may think of several purposes and mention them briefly. A major purpose may have been to make public the transfer of authority to Solomon and his constituency. The tone is almost that of a marriage: a king being married to his people.

Q9. Let group members list the points found in verses 6–10. Then discuss the principles that grow out of these instructions.

Q10. See verses 19–21 along with any other ways that group members notice in the passage.

Q11. If your group is slow to respond to this, ask, "According to this prayer, what kinds of things belong to God?"

Answers should include: God is ruler of all things, everything belongs to Him already (power, riches, abilities), we give back to Him only what was His from the beginning.

Q12. Be sure that people understand the major emphasis of David's prayer before proceeding to this question.

Q13. Treat this question briefly if time is limited. You might mention that the apostle Paul described David as "a man after God's own heart" (Acts 13:22).

Q14, 15. Encourage as many as are willing to speak openly to these questions.

16 / WHAT WAS DAVID'S PHILOSOPHY OF LIFE?

Psalm 139

Q2. See verses 4 and 6.

Q3. Encourage several responses to the first part of this question. Clues to David's attitude appear in verses 5 and 6.

Q4. The previous stanza spoke of God being all-knowing. This stanza says He is everywhere present.

Q7. See verse 13 in answer to the first question. Spend a few moments discussing the second half, emphasizing particularly verse 14, "I praise you because I am fearfully and wonderfully made; your works are wonderful." (NIV)

Q8. Don't encourage revelations that are too private here. (A note of humor will help.) Instead emphasize positive effects these verses can have on the way we deal with good and bad traits in ourselves.

Q9. See verses 15, "My frame was not hidden from you," and 16, "All the days ordained for me were written in your book before one of them came to be." Then let people link these truths with their own feelings about sickness and death.

Q10. Verse 17 implies that God allows us to know some of His thoughts, else how could David call them "precious." Yet the rest of the stanza implies God's unknowability. God's thoughts are more vast than we can count.

Q11. At this point, the psalm takes an abrupt change in tone and direction—a shift difficult for most readers to follow. It seems that David, in his writing, has become so moved by God's enormity, His goodness, His personal love, that a brief look at "the wicked" sends him crashing over to God's side because of the awful contrast. David sees God's enemies as his own enemies.

Groups who have trouble with these verses might do well to remember that while God commanded Old Testament readers not to mistreat their enemies (see Lesson 13) "Love your enemies" is a New Testament command initiated by Jesus in Matthew 5:43–44.

Q13. Verses 1–18 look up at God; verses 19–22 look out at the wicked; but in verses 23–24, David looks inside himself.

Notes on question 11 discuss the change in perspective between the first two parts. It seems only natural that David, after his scathing accusation of the wicked, would point the finger back to himself and ask if there is any part of himself joining the wicked in their opposition to a holy God.

Q14. Select an expressive reader to read the entire poem aloud before discussing the final three questions.

If the term "philosophy of life" bothers some members, ask "What does David believe to be true about God, life, himself?"

Q15. If necessary review verses that reflect David's feelings about the qualities that he describes in God. Verses 5, 6, 10, 14, 17 might help.

BIBLIOGRAPHY

Blaikie, W. G. *The First Book of Samuel*. New York: A. C. Armstrong & Son, 1887. Reprinted by Klock and Klock, 1978.

Blaikie, W. G. *The Second Book of Samuel*. New York: A. C. Armstrong & Son, 1887. Reprinted by Klock and Klock, 1978.

Bonhoeffer, Dietrich. *Psalms: The Prayer Book of the Bible*. Minneapolis: Augsburg, 1970.

Douglas, J. D. *New Bible Dictionary*. Grand Rapids: Eerdmans, 1962.

Edersheim, Alfred. *Old Testament Bible History*. Grand Rapids: Eerdmans, 1954.

Gulston, Charles. *David: Shepherd and King*. Grand Rapids: Zondervan, 1980.

Guthrie, D., J. A. Motyer, A. M. Stibbs, D. J. Wiseman. *New Bible Commentary*. Grand Rapids: Eerdmans, 1970.

Henry, Matthew. *Commentary on the Whole Bible*. 6 vols. Vol. 2. Old Tappan: Fleming H. Revell Company, reprint ed.

Keil, C. F. and F. Delitzsch. *Commentary on the Old Testament*. Grand Rapids: Eerdmans. Reprinted 1976.

Lewis, C. S. *Reflections on the Psalms*. New York: Harcourt, Brace, and World, 1958.

May, Herbert G., editor. *Oxford Bible Atlas*. Second edition. London and New York: Oxford University Press, 1974.

Maclaren, Alexander. *Expositions of Holy Scripture*. 17 vols. Vol. 2. Grand Rapids: Baker Book House. Reprinted 1974.

Pfeiffer, Charles F. and Everett F. Harrison. *Wycliffe Bible Commentary*. Chicago: Moody Press, 1962.

Ryken, Leland. *The Literature of the Bible*. Grand Rapids: Zondervan, 1974.

Scott, Jack B. *An Old Testament Survey: God's Plan Unfolded*. Wheaton: Tyndale, 1978.

Youngman, Bernard R. Edited by Walter Russell Bowie. *The Lands and People of the Living Bible*. New York: Hawthorne Books, 1959.

AN INDEX OF DAVID'S PSALMS AND "THROUGH THE WEEK" NARRATIVE

Psalm	Lesson	Psalm	Lesson	Psalm	Lesson
3	12	35	13	110	15
4	12	36	2	122	14
5	11	37	15	124	2
6	10	38	14	131	2
7	6	39	15	133	5
8	15	40	7	138	8
9	13	41	12	139	16
11	3	51	10	140	4
12	11	52	3	141	1
13	15	53	2	142	4
14	2	54	5	143	5
15	8	55	12	144	7
16	9	56	3	145	9
17	5	57	4		
18	9	58	13	1 Samuel	Lesson
19	1	59	3	15	1
20	15	60	9	18–19	2
21	7	61	7	21–22	3
22	10	62	5	26–30	6
23	1	63	12		
24	8	64	5	2 Samuel	
25	14	65	7		
26	4	68	8	2–5	7
27	8	69	13	8–10	9
28	11	70	5	13–14	11
29	2	86	4	17	12
30	8	101	6	19:9–21:22	13
31	14	103	9, 11	22–23	14
32	11	108	14		
34	3	109	13		